Frontispiece: Welcome to the Black Country!

BEST
PUB WALKS
in
THE BLACK COUNTRY

Chris Rushton

Published by Sigma Leisure – an imprint of
Sigma Press, 1 South Oak Lane, Wilmslow, Cheshire SK9 6AR, England.

British Library Cataloguing in Publication Data
A CIP record for this book is available from the British Library.

ISBN: 1-85058-416-8

Typesetting and Design by: Sigma Press, Wilmslow, Cheshire.

Cover: Sarah Hughes Brewery (Chris Rushton)

Printed by: Manchester Free Press

Acknowledgment: my very grateful thanks go to Les Lumsdon, my walking companion, for his extensive research in preparing this book, for accompanying me on all the walks, including visiting the pubs and sampling the ales!

Foreword

When you think about rambling and real ales in the Black Country the image is of plenty of choice of the latter but walks limited to excursions around relics of our industrial past some of which are still in full operation. What surprises people about the area is how many green lungs there have always been and how many industrial sites have been restored to nature.

While canal towpaths and old railway lines cut through the whole of the region, farming and nature have been preserved in such areas as Sedgley Beacon (highest farm land between here and the Urals), Sandwell Valley, Saltwells, Cotwell End, etc. The image of industrial grime also belies the Black Country's location on the edge of the scenic countryside with Kinver Edge, the Clent Hills, Highgate Common, and Cannock Chase all pressing against the urban area.

The Black Country's reputation for drinking choice is rightfuly famous. We are probably the world's best known area for mild beer, and our style of bitter with its sweet, hoppy flavours is also renowned. The Black Country's reputation for choice and cheapness is probably due to the competition which exists between the small, regional breweries.

Unlike most other areas of the country, the big brewers have never found themselves in anything like the monopoly position. Local independents like Banks's and Hansons, Bathams (see picture, next page) and Holdens have a well-deserved following for the excellent, well-priced beers. A new generation of micro brewers has maintained that choice through the opening of British Oak, Enville and the re-opening of the historic Sarah Hughes

Brewery at Sedgley. Even some of the national brewers seem to have become imbued with the Black Country spirit with Carlsberg Tetley opening a new brewery – Holt, Plant & Deakin at Wolverhampton. Bass have preserved the wonderful Highgate Brewery at Walsall, probably the only all-Mild brewery in the world.

Sadly, we have not completely escaped the ravages of brewery closures with the much-loved Simpkiss being closed by Greenhall Whitley, Springfield by Bass, Julia Hanson by Woverhampton and Dudley (Banks's), all within the last decade. The historic brewhouse, "Ma Pardoes" at Netherton, regretfully remains idle at the time of writing, despite promises to re-open it.

Nevertheless, the Black Country still has nine working breweries and another 16 within 20 miles of its borders. The pubs in the Black Country are surprisingly varied with many hidden gems. Usually the more they have been ignored by the brewery the better they are. Handpumps are replacing increasingly electric pumps as the preferred dispensing method of serving real ale. Keg pubs have always been hard to find in the Black Country and continue to be so. If it is not a handpump on the bar then ask, but it is almost certainly still going to be real ale in these parts.

The Black Country is unique and the best way to savour it is on foot with regular stops to quench your thirst at the focal point of the community – its local pub. Good walking and good drinking! The Black Country is the place to enjoy both.

Bob Jones; Chairman, CAMRA Black Country

Tim Batham, Batham's Brewery, Delph

CONTENTS

Distance: 3 miles

Distance: 3 miles

Distance: 3 miles

Distance: 5 miles

Distance: 3 miles

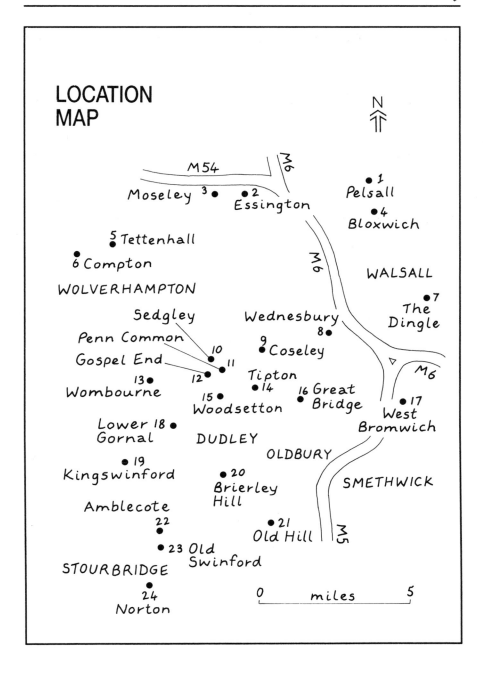

LOCATION
MAP

N
⇑

M54   M6

Moseley 3●   ●2   Pelsall ●1
            Essington   ●4
                            Bloxwich

5● Tettenhall
●
6 Compton   M6

WOLVERHAMPTON   WALSALL
                                        ●7
      Sedgley   Wednesbury   The
                          8●   Dingle
Penn Common   9
Gospel End   10 ●Coseley   ▽
          13● 11   M6
Wombourne 12●   Tipton
              15● ●14   ●17
          Woodsetton 16●Great   West
                          Bridge   Bromwich
Lower 18 ●
Gornal   DUDLEY
                    OLDBURY
    ●19
Kingswinford   ●20   SMETHWICK
            Brierley
Amblecote   Hill
    22   M5
    ●   ●21
    ●23 Old   Old Hill
STOURBRIDGE Swinford
    24   0   miles   5
Norton

INTRODUCTION

Like many other books this one does not indicate where, exactly, the Black Country is. The map provides a rough guideline as does the selection of walks, but the Black Country is best described as a place which defies rigid geographical definition. It is as much about a people and their communities as physical boundaries. One thing is for certain, however: it is placed geographically in a basin which is divided by a central ridge running east-west for approximately seven miles between the edges of Rowley Regis and Sedgley.

There are few rivers and none of significance. They drain away from the watershed ridge, the Tame to the north and the Stour towards the Severn. The importance of water in the Black Country lies moreso in the canal network.

It is difficult to imagine that prior to the 19th century the area to the north and west of Birmingham was predominantly rural with a scattering of small commercial towns such as Wolverhampton and Walsall, Dudley and Stourbridge. By the middle of the century the growth of industry and population had changed the landscape completely. This place became known world-wide as the Black Country and the image of blackness by day and red by night known to all who could read the vivid descriptions by the travelling scribes of the day.

Skills and trades

Of course, development was slower than the term 'industrial revolution' suggests. The South Staffordshire coalfield had been important since Tudor times and quarrying for lime and minerals similarly. The skills and trades built up through the centuries should not be dismissed either. Blacksmiths and nail makers, saddlers and the like became important and places hereabouts gained a reputation for such trades as locksmithing, and leather working.

But the changes of the late eighteenth century were far more significant. It was the combination of the proximity of raw materials and technological break-throughs in smelting and the production of wrought iron that brought rapid economic growth. Abraham Derby's successful attempts to coke coal for blast furnaces instead of wood charcoal brought immense benefits to those working in iron. Furthermore, the installation of steam power at industrial works meant considerable increases in production. Estimates vary but it is thought that in the early years of the 19th century there were between 40 and 50 blast furnaces in the Black Country.

At the same time the canal network was being developed at a pace. Within a period of 50 to 60 years a network of canals had been built, navigations to bring in raw materials and ship out finished goods hence a network of waterways which allowed unrivalled access to so many pits, furnaces and works. They were superseded by an equally dense pattern of railways but until the early decades of the 20th century, canals very much held their own in these parts.

Poems and Pubs

Such rapid industrialisation attracted a work force which lived close by and hence the Black Country became a sea of terraced housing. Villages and towns merged together in an urban sprawl and during this era the poverty of the work force became all too apparent to the visitor. It was also a time when strong cultural ties were established; ways of doing things, poems and pub talk, work skills and customs developed. One such custom was the breeding of fighting dogs. It was in Cradley Heath, for example, that the Staffordshire Bull Terrier was reared, a cross between the English Terrier and a Bulldog. The breed was used as a pit dog and several champions became legendary such as Champion Gentleman Jim. Part of the Black Country culture remains to this day.

The Black Country Museum

Much of the early industrial building has gone but there are reminders, the Black Country Museum being an outstanding example. This portrays life as it would have been in the Black Country during the past two hundred years. The museum site was part of the Earl of Dudley's industrial empire and dozens of mines would have been sunk here as well as workings for coal, limestone and clay. This is reflected in the old mine and there is also a replica of a Newcomen engine used for pumping water from the early pits.

The Black Country Museum

The heart of the museum is the village where actors and actresses bring the buildings to life – the baker's shop, chemists, chain-maker's house and the Bottle and Glass public house. The latter has been re-built here alongside the Dudley Canal. It was originally at Buckpool near Brierley Hill (not far from the Brierley Hill walk).

There are also boat trips into the complex of canals beneath Dudley. This was originally built to transport from the huge excavated caverns limestone to other parts of the Black Country. There were no towpaths here as in the Netherton Tunnel so the boatmen had to leg their boats through the tunnel or employ leggers to do the job for them. The horses were taken overland.

There are many museums and industrial sites throughout the Black Country which celebrate the skills and crafts of the area such as The Leather Museum mentioned in the Dingle Ramble at Walsall. The Lock Museum at Willenhall, for example, illustrates the growth of the lock industry in the last century. The museum is sited in a Victorian Locksmith's house where gas lit rooms contains artefacts belonging to a locksmith of the last century. But there are other little gems to discover, the Mushroom Green Chainshop at Dudley Wood where the skill of the Victorian chain maker are shown, and the Red House Glass Cone at Amblecote.

Glassmaking

The Glass industry has always been concentrated more in the Stour valley and was no doubt stimulated by the arrival of the Stourbridge Canal. The concentration of the glass industry in and around Stourbridge remains to this day and the Amblecote ramble highlights a number of places to visit.

The Red House Glassworks Museum at Stuart Crystal, Stourbridge

Canal Heritage

Several museums reflect the Black Country's canals including the Birchills Canal Museum at Walsall. Canals are undeniably one of the strongest features on the Black Country landscape. The canal era had a greater impact here than anywhere in the country. Such navigations not only linked coalfield with furnace but brought together village and town and even created new settlements such as Dudley Port. The great canal engineers worked here too. Brindley engineered the Staffordshire and Worcester, and became involved with the old main line between Birmingham and Wolverhampton. Telford came later but had a major involvement with many of the region's navigations including such great engineering feats as the Dudley and Netherton tunnels.

The Black Country canal system is part of the Birmingham Canal Navigations (often referred to by the abbreviation of BCN) and what survives is a tribute to the architectural richness of the designs with locks and wharves, red brick and ornate iron bridges bringing relief to an industrial background.

Sadly, many of the smaller wharves and branches have been filled in, but there are constant reminders of their existence as you tread the towpaths. Charles Hadfield's early book *Canals in the West Midlands* listed 60 canals in the BCN network and it is unfortunate that by the mid-1960s half had been abandoned. Since then matters have changed and the canals are now heralded as green lungs. The investment in the Birmingham to Wolverhampton main-line cana is a classic example with improved towpaths, restored bridges and buildings as well as an imaginative use as a Black Country cycleway. Let's hope that lesser known canals receive similar attention. The book introduces the would be walker to many fascinating sections of navigation in the area.

Dudley is, for many, the centre of the Black Country and is very much a historic site, known for its lords rather than industrial past. The historian, D.M. Pallister, writing in *The Staffordshire Landscape* emphasises the importance of the Lords of Dudley:

Industrial Reflections on the Stourbridge Branch Canal

"Standing in the Market Place, even today one can sense this crucial fact. To the north-east along Castle Street, past St Edmund's church, the view is dominated by the castle on its hill, while in the opposite direction High Street leads up to the spire of St Thomas. Here one is standing in the Lord's market-place and between the Lord's churches . . ."

The original castle works date from the 11th century and the site has been used as a fortress and then a dwelling by a succession of earls for many centuries. It is now the home of Dudley Zoo and Castle. But the Lords of Dudley had considerable influence in the Black Country, not only through their extensive ownership of estates but through their quest for improved canals and railways to exploit local mineral reserves, regardless of the impact on the environment.

Dudley suffered a tumultuous change with the rise of the coal mining and metal working sectors. Industrial giants of the time such as the Foleys of Birmingham set down a pattern of larger scale works and while most have now gone the legacy of their existence shapes the way of life here. Dudley retains a pedestrianised shopping area and street market and is the home of a very successful beer festival every year around Spring Bank Holiday time.

The Pubs

One of the great joys of walking in the Black Country is the option to call into a local hostelry for a good pint of ale (or other beverage) either at the end of the day or at a lunch break. Many of the inns and pubs featured in this book have throughout the centuries welcomed the traveller on foot, miners and quarrymen going to or from their daily work as well as the coach traveller of the last century journeying to and from the major centres of commercial activity. Of course, journey times were far longer even on horseback and staying at an inn overnight was a very common occurrence if you had the where-with-all.

The Old Swan (Ma Pardoe's): Netherton, Dudley

Most of the pubs mentioned in this book were built (or re-built) in the last century to serve the growing population who came to work in the foundries or on the canals. They were community ale houses and the clientele would have been very local indeed. Mild became the preferred drink hereabouts and many of the pubs would have been brew houses as well as retailing local ales.

The pubs have changed, some more than others. Most still serve a predominantly local trade but the importance of heavy manufacturing and mining has declined dramatically. Thus, the pubs now seek to serve the new leisure markets rather than the thousands that were finishing shifts at all hours of the day.

Publicans in the Black Country usually have a welcome for all comers. That is their reputation and ramblers, boaters and the like are no exception. The vast majority of the pubs mentioned in this book have been approached by the author to ensure that details of opening times and the like are accurate at the time of writing.

Many pubs and especially those country pubs mentioned have changed in the past two to three decades to meet the needs of the new markets. The first major change is that many pubs serve food and this has become so important to their trading that publicans only allow people, ramblers or otherwise, to eat food bought on their premises. Most of the pubs in this book offer bar meals at lunch and in the evening but it is not usually the entire session, more likely to be noon until 2pm and from 7pm until 9 to 9.30pm. Unless stated in the text the pub concerned does not allow eating your own (food that is) on the premises.

The same applies to muddy boots. Publicans would prefer you to leave them outside. Most pubs now have no bar with tiled or wooden floors where boots and wellies are accepted. Most rooms tend to be carpeted. Thus, it makes sense to kick off your boots before entering to avoid the offence of being asked to do this. Clean trainer shoes are obviously no problem and most of these walks will be easy to walk wearing trainers during summer months when it is drier. This is not the case in the winter when towpaths and bridleways in particular get very muddy.

The question of families in pubs often arises. Most publicans in the book are happy to welcome families, especially if children are well behaved. Most have gardens or outdoor seats for summer use and this is ideal for the family group. Children are also welcome indoors if there is a separate area or room away from the bar. This is the law. Thus, it makes sense for mum or dad to simply pop a head around the door to ask whether it is all right to bring the family in! Some hostelries feel they are not geared up for families at all and say so. It is not that children are not welcome, it is simply whether facilities are available or not.

One thing is for certain, the tradition of hospitality and keeping good beer remains as strong as ever in the Black Country. The choice of beers is excellent and beers at an affordable price. The author thanks The Campaign For Real Ale (CAMRA), which has for the past two decades championed the cause of the real ale drinker and the retention of characterful local pubs. Interested readers should contact CAMRA, 34 Alma Road, St Albans.

There is a hitch, of course, for the rambler who loves real ale. Beer and driving do not mix at all. Every ramble in this book features a pub and several mention two or more *en route*. Those readers who find it impossible to pass a pub without sampling a glass or two, should let someone else do the driving. Better still, do as the author did when researching this volume – use a local bus or train whenever possible. It helps to keep congestion down and puts money into a vital local facility.

The Walks

The 24 walks vary in length from three to eight miles and are all easy going, as there are not many hills to climb. They are, for the most part, three to five miles in length, just enough to whet the appetite for a spot of refreshment. Pace yourselves on these, for there are no medals for coming first.

It goes without saying that you should not trust the weather. Always go prepared with a waterproof. It is easy enough to take a light rucksack with a jumper and outer garment. The walks should be easy to follow by simply using a good map and the instructions in the book. There tends to be two main problems regarding instructions for the reader. The first relates to how the author perceives the route and describes it. If you find yourself off the prescribed route, retrace your steps to a point where you found the text to be absolutely clear and then look again at the points mentioned by the author to aid navigation. I realise that you might curse me on occasion!

The second point relates to when things change. As the country-side is a working environment field patterns, areas of woodland and buildings change. Please accept our apologies in advance for this. The text has been written so that even if a hedge is grubbed or housing built, the way should still be easy to follow.

The Black Country Museum: will the trams return?

Getting About

Public transport in the Black Country is good in comparison to most places. The rail network out of Birmingham and Wolver-hampton to some destinations such as Tipton and Coseley is a real benefit. The 'Countrygoer' concept of using buses and trains to get into the countryside wherever you can is one which the author endorses. It can enhance the fun of the outing, reduces environmental intrusion and the risk of car theft as well as helping to support local services. West Midlands Centro produce excellent public transport maps and timetable information can be obtained by 'phoning or by calling into local travel information offices.

The Black Country has much to offer those seeking walks with a difference. These are walks steeped in industrial heritage where the prospect of good ale in characterful public houses and a welcome as genuine as the guidebooks suggest will have you returning time and time again. Good walking and raise a glass or two to the Black Country when you are there. It is a place to be cherished.

Tourist Information

Please check opening times of the museums and other attractions mentioned in the book by contacting one of the following Tourist Information Offices:

Dudley Tourist Information Centre (0384) 250333

Wolverhampton Tourist Information Centre (0902) 312051

Public transport

For details of public transport services make a call to the Centro Hotline on 021 200 2700. Centro also produces excellent maps and information leaflets.

Black Country Beers

Real ale is a draught beer made from natural ingredients, matured in a cask where secondary fermentation takes place, and dispensed without the use of carbon dioxide (other than that naturally produced). The beer is sometimes referred to as cask-conditioned as indicated on many of the Banks's Brewery electrically powered dispensers to be found in some of their houses. Many pubs now draw the beers from the cask through hand-pumps and in rare instances the ale is drawn straight from the cask.

The scope of this book is not to re-write the entire history and process of brewing. This type of detail can be read elsewhere and you would find a copy of the Good Beer Guide, published by CAMRA on an annual basis, very helpful in this respect. The Black Country is, however, known for its exceptional beers, and therefore you will find below an easy to read section on the major brews available in the locality!

The CAMRA guide to the Black Country, available at local shops, is a must!

The Breweries and their Brews

Bathams Delph Brewery, Brierley Hill

The brewery stands adjacent to The Vine pub (see the Brierley Hill ramble), an independent family concern which has been brewing since 1877. *The History of Batham's, Black Country Brewers* by John Richards records that the Batham family in the early 19th century were nailmakers. By the 1880s Daniel Batham and Charlotte Batham had taken up brewing on a commercial level at the White Horse Inn at Cradley. Throughout the remainder of their life they lay the foundations of Batham's Black Country Brewery, an establishment much loved by real ale drinkers of the 1990s.

Batham's brewery is certainly growing from strength to strength. In the earlier years the brewery was renowned for its dark mild beers and this is where success lay. Mild beers accounted for most of the production. Now the reverse is true, Batham's Best Bitter dominates but Mild Ale is still important and is enjoying something of a come-back in a gentle way.

The brews are Mild Ale (Original Gravity 1037) and Best Bitter (Original Gravity 1044), and XXX – a Christmas ale (OG 1064). They are brewed under the supervision of Tim Batham and his head brewer in the heart of the Black Country.

Banks's (also known as The Wolverhampton and Dudley Breweries), Wolverhampton

The smell of Banks's beers often drifts across Wolverhampton when a batch brew is on the way. Banks's is by far the largest regional brewery in the Midlands (said to be producing half a million barrels of the good stuff a year), and has extended its influence in recent years by purchasing Camerons at Hartlepool. It has secured an interesting deal with Marston's Brewery in Burton whereby Banks's Mild is sold in their houses in return for Marston's Pedigree in Banks's pubs.

What is so pleasing about Banks's brewery is that it has backed mild beers consistently during a decade when mild has been losing its popularity. Mild accounts for well over 50 percent of cask conditioned production at Wolverhampton. The brewery also promotes the beer unlike many of its competitors! Banks's Mild is well recognised as a quality drink so let us hope that it continues to hold its own in an increasingly competitive marketplace. Banks's took over Julia Hanson's brewery at Dudley during the Second World War but unfortunately closed it down in 1991 much to the dismay of local drinkers.

The range of beers is:

Hanson's Mild	(OG 1033)
Banks's Mild	(OG 1036)
Bitter	(OG 1038)

British Oak, Dudley

This micro brewery is situated at the British Oak public house at Eve Hill, Dudley and on the pub exterior you will see the words Skittain ales which is an anagram of the brewer's name. One mildly frustrating admission is that on occasions the brewery tap runs out of the beer and on more than one excursion Tetley Bitter has been the only real ale on offer.

The brew is available at other outlets so keep your eyes peeled for Eve'll Bitter (OG 1042) and there is now British Oak Mild available.

Holden's Brewery, Woodsetton

Like Bathams this is one of truly independent Black Country family breweries which make the area such an enjoyable place to imbibe. The brewery began life at the Park Inn, now the brewery tap, and has expanded somewhat over the years on an adjacent site. It is estimated to produce approximately 9000 barrels per annum and 25-30 percent is estimated to be Mild, the remainder Bitters and an old ale.

Years back Bathams and Holdens held discussions to explore the possibility of a merger. The talks petered out and thankfully we still have two excellent breweries competing in the Black Country. Holdens has more tied houses than Bathams but between them they offer a choice of quality beers at reasonable prices.

Holdens' beers are:

Mild	(OG 1037)
Bitter	(OG 1039)
XB	(OG 1042) Sometimes referred to as Lucy B.
Special	(OG 1052)
XL	(OG 1092) A strong Christmas Ale

Pitfield, Stourbridge

The brand names Pitfield and Premier beers belong to the Chain-maker Beer Company which now falls under the banner of the much larger UB Group. Pitfield Mild (OG 1035) and Bitter (OG 1036) are available at the Old Swan in Netherton and other outlets.

Sarah Hughes, Sedgley

The brews come from a restored tower brewhouse to the rear of the Beacon Hotel where brewer Lee Cox brews using a recipe which previous owner Sarah Hughes developed in the earlier decades of the century.

The current owner, John Hughes decided to start brewing again in 1987 after a lapse of almost 30 years on the site. The attention to detail and quality of ingredients mean that Sarah Hughes Mild is an extraordinary beer with a powerful edge to it. It certainly has revived the fortunes of the traditional strong Black Country Mild which would have been the norm years ago. Ironically, much of the Mild is sold in other parts of the country through wholesalers. It is very much an envoy for Black Country beer but there's nowhere better to sample it than on home ground. There are other outlets such as Crown and Cushion at Ocker Hill where the landlord sells the tasty beverage as a guest ale in his Holt, Plant and Deakin pub.

The beers are:

Sedgley Surprise Bitter	(OG 1048)
Original Dark Ruby Mild	(OG 1058)

National breweries:

Bass

M&B Mild, Charrington IPA and M&B Brew XI. The Walsall brewery at Highgate deserves special mention as it produces M&B Highgate Dark (but everyone still asks for it by its old name of Highgate Mild). This brewery also produces a winter brew, Old Ale.

Carlsberg-Tetley

One of the subsidiaries of this giant is Holt, Plant and Deakin from Wolverhampton, a Black Country based company which is popular. The Entire is still brewed in the Black Country but ironically the Mild and Bitter now come from Warrington in Cheshire!

The other national brewers such as Courage, Whitbread and Scottish & Newcastle are represented throughout the Midlands but fortunately do not overwhelm the Black Country.

1. PELSALL

Route: York's Bridge — Pelsall Junction — Wyrley Common Bridge — Wyrley Common — High Bridge — York's Bridge

Distance: 3 miles

Map: O.S. Pathfinder Sheet 913 Lichfield and Brownhills

Start: The Royal Oak, York's Bridge

Access: There are numerous buses out of Walsall Bus Station for Brownhills and Cannock via Pelsall. You need to ask for Norton Lane and there is a stop before the junction of the Wolverhampton and Lichfield roads.

Travel north on the B4154 through Pelsall to Norton Lane. It is difficult to park in Norton Lane so park near Pelsall Common and walk the last stretch up to Norton Lane.

The Royal Oak, Pelsall. Tel (0922) 691811.

This is a popular spot, especially the common to the rear of the pub by the canal. The Royal Oak offers the Ansells range of traditional beers, Mild, Bitter and Burton Ale, on handpull. It has a lounge and a restaurant and meals are served during all sessions. The Royal Oak is open from 11am until 3pm at lunchtimes and from 7pm in the evenings. Usual Sunday opening times.

Walsall

In recent years, Walsall has gained a reputation for its illuminations which run from mid-September through to the last week of

October and there's even a tongue-in-cheek Black Country Seaside Special evening out. People travel from miles around for "Pier Style" entertainment in the company of a number of celebrated Black Country comedians. The illuminations are based on Walsall's famous arboretum, a 19th century creation which has been retained for recreation. Walsall has seen many changes with the building of intrusive roads and characterless shopping precincts but it still retains pockets of architectural glory such as the County Court area.

Walsall Canal Museum

The town also has a number of exceptional museums such as the Walsall Leather Museum where you can see first hand the craft and skill of the leather trade for which the area is renowned. Not only are there demonstrations but you can buy goods at the museum shop too! The museum is in Wisemore, about ten minutes walk from the centre.

Those interested in canal heritage should call into the Birchills canal museum to be found at the top lock of the eight flight near to the centre. The museum was originally a small Boatmen's Mission dating from the turn of the century with an aim of improving the lot of the folk who worked on the canals. It also sought to draw poor souls from the less savoury aspects of life into purer ways. It now houses exhibitions about life on the canals. There's also a Walsall Canal Trail from here which is much enhanced by a booklet (small charge) which provides information about buildings surrounding the canals in the town.

Not many people know that Walsall is the birthplace of Jerome K Jerome, whose most famous work *Three Men in a Boat* is read by young scholars throughout the world. His birthplace in Belsize House, Bradford Street has been restored as a small museum reflecting on his life and works. This is a must for those who enjoy literature. You might also take a look at the Garman Ryan collection of paintings, drawings and sculpture at the Walsall Museum and Art Gallery in Lichfield Street.

Pelsall

The immediate impression gained in Pelsall is one of wide flowing greens which give it a feeling of spaciousness. Nearby stands the red brick parish church which dates mainly from the last century and contains several interesting monuments to local families.

On the walk it is interesting to note the different styles of canal building. The earlier Essington and Wyrley Canal follows the contours and hence winds its way through the urban development whilst the Cannock Extension, which was built in the 1860s runs straight through to Chasewater.

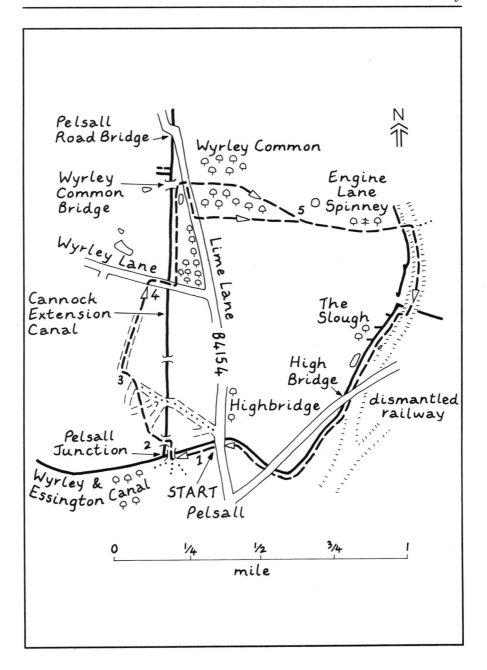

On the return leg of the walk, you will notice Clayhanger Common to your left, a site reclaimed in recent years by Walsall Borough Council. Prior to industrialisation it would have been rough pasture on the edges of the Royal Forest of Cannock. Enclosure for farming and subsequent extraction of clay (as the name suggests) brought many changes and since the site has been used for infill of varying descriptions. Remarkably, it is now recovering as a site for leisure as nature re-establishes with a little help from the rangers. There is a nature trail and leaflet explaining the flora and wildlife of the area.

The Walk

1. Walk to the left of the Royal Oak across the common to the canal towpath and make your way up to Pelsall Junction, a remote area where the outline of the Victorian canal architecture is accentuated by the surrounding low-lying heathland. The effect is the feeling of remoteness which is unusual in these parts.

2. Cross the iron bridge and over the Friar Bridge which spans the Cannock Extension canal. Here you are confronted by four paths. Take the one on the right but still moving away from the towpath. Within 20 metres it narrows and forks again. Bear right here along a path which is not clear on the ground. Your target is a footpath sign which is ahead. You will see another bridge over the canal to your right. Some people simply follow the towpath to this bridge and cut left and almost immediately right along a hedge to the very same sign.

3. Either way, you reach the footpath sign by a hedge. Cross the stile here and bear slightly right to join an old track surrounded by hawthorns. This leads to another stile. Go over it and turn right. You reach a third stile which is crossed and then proceed across the field to a road.

4. Go right to the canal bridge and turn left to wander down to the towpath and ahead. You pass by a pool on the right and then at the next bridge go right up the embankment to join an old track. Turn right to pass the kennels on your right. Go over the main road and walk ahead into Wryley Common, where scrub is re-colonising a one time mine. You can see the remains of the old track bed of the railway. This soon bears right and climbs through old spoil heaps, eventually dropping down a bank to the corner of the wood. The way is shredded by cycle and motorcycle tracks. There is an alternative. Instead of crossing over at the main road, go right to pass houses. Cross the road and at the wood's edge go left along a track which more or less follows the perimeter fence.

5. Either way you join an old track known appropriately as Engine Lane. You pass Engine Lane spinney on your left and then come to an old canal spur, bereft of water now. Just beyond is the trackbed of a Staffordshire railway line.

   Drop down onto it and turn left. It runs through to Clayhanger Common. On reaching the canal bridge you go right down to the canal towpath. Walk ahead as the canal bends sharp left at what was once a junction. This soon passes beneath High Bridge and winds its way by houses back to York's Bridge and Pelsall Common where you return to The Royal Oak.

2. *ESSINGTON*

Route: Essington church — Essington Hall — Blackhalve Lane — Essington church

Distance: 3 miles

Map: O.S. Pathfinder Sheet 891 Wolverhampton (North)

Start: Essington Church

Access: Travel north on the A460 or A462 road and look for the B4156 which runs through Essington. There is limited on-street parking in the village. Essington is served by buses from Wolverhampton.

The Minerva, Wolverhampton Road. Tel: (0922) 405641

The Minerva is very much a local's pub and you will find people busily playing darts, dominoes and pool here. To the left is the bar cum games area and on the right an open lounge. On tap is the Ansell's range of draught beers in excellent condition. The Minerva is open at lunchtimes until 3pm and from early evening. Usual Sunday hours prevail.

Essington

The village of Essington lies amid the old coalfield and people from here worked in local pits such as Hilton Park Colliery. It has a modern brick church dating from the 1930s on what is the village main street with a few shops and the Minerva public house. Essington is now very much a dormitory village with people working in the nearby towns.

The mining industry still continues here and this has a short term detrimental effect on the landscape. Look out for diversions of footpaths on the route!

The Minerva, Essington

The Walk

1. Turn right from the gates of the church to walk down the Wolverhampton Road. The Minerva stands on your left and opposite the chemist's shop is a path. Follow this into an estate. Turn left and then right by houses. Cross the road and turn right and then first left to pass by garages to join a welcome path leading out into the countryside.

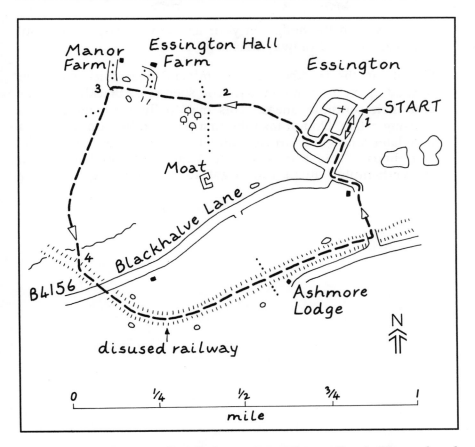

2. This runs between fields to a piece of woodland. Keep ahead
   here, ignoring all paths to the left and right. The path comes to
   a corner and the track bears right. You go ahead through a stile
   and into a field. Essington Hall Farm stands to the right across
   a field. Walk by what is probably the remains of a grubbed
   hedge to double gates beyond a barn belonging to Manor
   Farm.

3. You go left here by a tree and follow an old hedgerow. There's
   open cast quarrying here and this is the cause of diversions of
   footpaths in the vicinity. Your way is easy enough. You keep

company with the hedge on your left down a large field until you reach the old railway track.

4. Go left on the trackbed, an old mineral line which has been opened up for recreational use. You soon cross Blackhalve Lane and then continue ahead. This eventually runs alongside a housing estate. Do not take the first path left but a quarter of a mile later follow the tarmac path left through a park and by the club house. This brings you to High Hill. Go left and at Wolverhampton Road turn right to return to your starting point.

3. MOSELEY

Route: Northycote Country Park – Moseley Old Hall – Cannock Road – Northycote Country Park

Distance: 3 miles

Map: O.S. Pathfinder Sheet 891 Wolverhampton (North)

Start: Car Park, Northycote Country Park, off Northycote Lane

Access: Travel on the A460 and turn left at Underhill for Northycote Lane and Moseley

There are several buses from Wolverhampton to Northycote Lane. Contact the Centro Hotline on 021 200 2700.

The Anchor, Cross Green. Tel: (0902) 790466.

The Anchor is a very pleasant hostelry overlooking the Staffordshire and Worcestershire Canal, a mile north of Moseley. It has been attractively re-furbished with an unusual roof top drinking area from which there are good views of the surrounding countryside and the canal.

The Anchor serves the Ansells beers on handpull – Dark Mild, Ansells Bitter as well as Tetley Bitter and the ever popular Holts Entire. Food is available every lunch from noon until 2.30pm and from 6 to 9.30pm (10pm on Friday and Saturday). Families are welcome and there is good provision here for little ones including a play area.

The Anchor is open from noon until 3pm and from 6pm in the evening on weekdays and usual Sunday hours. It is a welcoming pub and walkers readily call in from the canalside. Join them!

Moseley Old Hall

Moseley Old Hall

Moseley Old Hall was built originally as a timber framed manor in the early years of the 17th century. It was here that Charles II took sanctuary in 1651 after being routed at the bloody battle of Worcester and the bed in which the good king is thought to have slept is said to be the one seen in the King's Room. There is a hiding place near to the splendid fireplace, with a secret door where those under persecution could hide away from predators.

There is so much more to see and gardens to treasure. You should set aside at least two hours to enjoy the hall. Moseley Old Hall is currently administered by the National Trust.

Northycote Farm, dating from the 17th century has been restored by Wolverhampton Borough as a working farm with a rural craft workshop, cafe and animals to see. A cottage garden is also being established.

The Walk

1. From the car park off Northycote Lane walk towards Northycote Farm but beforehand turn right to enter the country park. The track soon begins to descend, and as you near a bridge go left into wooded parkland.

2. The path proceeds through the woodland and then exits by way of a kissing gate. Turn right here and follow the old track into the dip where you will see Old Mill fish pond on your right, a quiet corner which attracts wildfowl. Rise up to Moseley Road. Turn right and walk to the turn to Moseley Old Hall. Go left to walk down to the Hall, if only to take a look at this historic building.

3. Return to the junction and now go left. Take care on this road as it is difficult to see oncoming traffic. The road soon dips down to a sharp right corner. You, however, continue ahead to

cross the fencing. Walk down the field and look for a stile on the left and a footbridge. Now go right up the field and cross a stile by a double gate.

4. Once on the road turn left and walk up to the main Cannock Road. Turn right to walk along the road until you reach a track on the right (signposted) which leads back to the park. You cross the bridge over the brook and then keep ahead once more to retrace your steps. Those who wish to extend the walk by a mile or so can bear left and follow some of the well marked trails throughout the park.

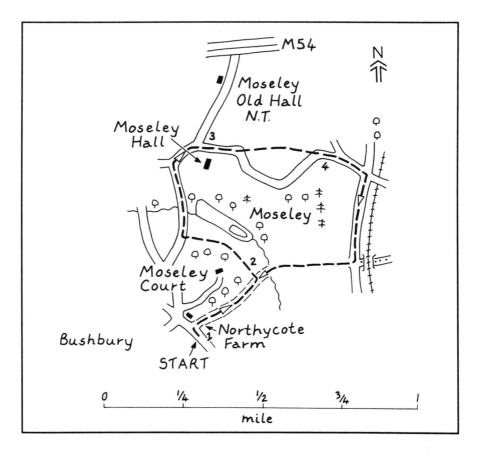

4. BLOXWICH

Route: Sneyd Wharf — Burnsnips Road — Springhill — Long Lane — Wyrley and Essington Canal — Sneyd Wharf

Distance: 5 miles

Map: O.S. Pathfinder Sheet 891 Wolverhampton (North)

Start: Sneyd Wharf, Bloxwich

Access: Sneyd Wharf is signposted off the A4124 off the Lichfield Road by the M6 motorway. There is a regular bus service along Lichfield Road.

The Why Not Inn, Springfield. Tel (0922) 496532

This village public house with an unusual front canopy offers shade and shelter throughout the year. Whilst having been refurbished in a mock heritage style, the Why Not offers a good pint of Banks's mild and bitter in warm surroundings; open from noon until 3pm at lunch and early evenings, this makes for a pleasant break half-way around the ramble. The Why Not is open all day Fridays and Saturdays. Children are welcome. Food is available at most times.

The Essington and Wyrley Canal

Built to link the Birmingham and Coventry canal in the late 18th century, this winding canal acts as a frontier between housing and countryside. It was built primarily for the shipment of coal and unfortunately fell into ruin after its abandonment in the 1950s.

The Why Not Inn

The Walk

1. Start at Sneyd Wharf, an increasingly popular centre for canal canoeing. Return to the main road, cross over and keep ahead along Vernon Way. Come to The Sneyd public house on the right and, as the road bends left, you keep ahead.

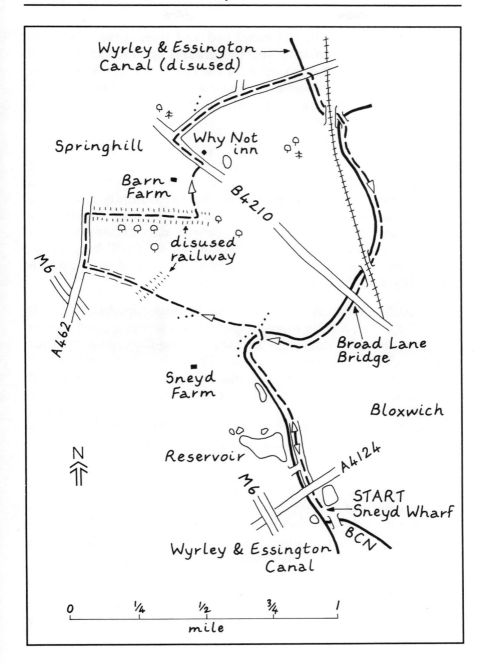

2. The path follows the old canal bed and then curves right. To your right is a grassland and the ground of Bloxwich Football Club. After the curve go left over the canal bed. In wet weather this may not be possible so you have to walk along a short distance, cross where drier and double back along the higher bank. Either way you join a track and you need to find a stile and sleeper bridge.

3. Go over both to enter reclaimed land, part of the old Sneyd mine and workings. There are hundreds of young trees planted in the area, presumably part of the new community forest. The idea of a new Forest of Mercia is an exciting one. Inspired by the Countryside Commission this project aims to bring together many organisations who will back a forest. It will be good to see them grow. Walk ahead between the rows of trees up to a track by a water course. Continue ahead.

4. The path eventually reaches the main Burnsnip Road. Go left for The Mitre, a large roadside pub which serves a good pint of mild. Otherwise turn right and walk along this awful road for just under one quarter of a mile. Then look for a stile on the right. The path is signposted and follows the course of an old dismantled railway. You will see a large gate ahead. This is not your way. Instead, look for a stile on the left, through a small plantation to cross another stile. The fenced path leads to a track where stiles are crossed by gates. Exit onto the main road in Springhill.

5. Opposite is the "Why Not" public house and why not indeed? Cross over and enter if in need of refreshment. Afterwards turn right out of the pub and right again into Long Lane. The name fits. It seems as if it is going to last forever. Ignore the turning left but keep ahead until you reach the canal bridge.

6. Turn right to join the towpath along a hauntingly beautiful section of the Wyrley and Essington Canal. It cuts left under the railway bridge and then runs to the right through low-lying

land. It can get wet along this section. The change comes when you cross Broad lane. The canal becomes dry and unfortunately litter becomes more prevalent as you follow the path to the rear of houses.

7. Re-join the section walked on the outward leg and return to Sneyd Wharf. What a contrasting walk!

5. TETTENHALL

Route: Tettenhall Road – Staffordshire and Worcestershire Canal – Aldersley Junction – Birmingham Canal – Wolverhampton

Distance: 3 miles

Map: O.S. Pathfinder sheets 891 Wolverhampton (North) and 912 Wolverhampton (South)

Start: Tettenhall Road (Canal Bridge)

Access: This is a linear route. Catch the bus to the start point, Tettenhall Road (A41), alighting at Meadow View, the stop before the junction with Henwood Road (B4161). Return on foot to Wolverhampton.

The Great Western. Tel: (0902) 351090

The Great Western is an institution. The local CAMRA group awarded it the status of "Pub of the Year" a couple of years ago and it is a *Good Beer Guide* entry. It stands beneath the complex of Wolverhampton Railway Station and opposite the old Wolverhampton Low Level. Throughout the last century this one-time ale house quenched the thirst of workers from local foundries and the railways. This is reflected in the railway memorabilia, mainly of Great Western origin as the pub's change of name recognises.

The Great Western has one central bar on a split level which serves several rooms. Families are welcome as there is an outdoor area to the rear and a marquee in the garden. Black Country ales are on handpull – Mild, Bitter and Lucy B from Holdens, Bathams Bitter and Bulmers traditional cider. Food is served at lunchtime and there are often rolls available early evening.

The Great Western

The Great Western is well worth finding, currently situated in a quiet nook near to the superbly restored Great Western Low Level Station. This area will not always be quiet as there are plans to introduce a light rail metro system between Wolverhampton, West Bromwich and Birmingham which will terminate here. The Great Western, in the meantime, is open from 11am until 11pm on Mondays to Fridays, 11am until 2.30pm and from 5.30pm on Saturdays. Sunday opening is noon until 2.30pm.

Wolverhampton

Standing on higher ground the town of Wolverhampton dates back to early times. It is said that the name derives from AD 985 when King Ethelred granted lands to Wulfrun. She funded what was to be a flourishing monastery here and established estates throughout South Staffordshire. It certainly had a market by 1180 and enjoyed a borough status through medieval times. A central core around St Peter's church, particularly street-names such as Cheapside and Exchange, survive.

Wolverhampton centre has been re-vitalised in recent years with buildings beautifully restored such as the distinctive Chubb Lock works. The central shopping area leads to the Wolverhampton Museum and Art Gallery where there is housed an extensive collection of British and North American "pop" art. There's also the Bantock House Museum in Bantock Park where enamels, porcelain, and a range of toys and dolls may be viewed.

The Walk

1. Catch a bus from Wolverhampton bus station along the Tettenhall Road, alighting at the stop before Henwood Road by the Toy Emporium. Walk down the little road by it, Meadow View, which bends right to Tettenhall old bridge across the canal. Go right to reach the towpath and keep ahead. The canal runs parallel with the old Kingswinford branch railway track-bed and Tettenhall station is a GWR survival worth a look.

2. This path runs beneath a wooded nature reserve and then you will see across the waters the modernised Wolverhampton Race Course at Dunstall Park. You reach Aldersley Junction where a distinctive sign offers direction to Stourport, Great Haywood and Birmingham. Go over the footbridge on the right and head for Birmingham.

3. Recent work on the canal has made it a very attractive green lung through an industrial zone. Oxley sidings stand to your left with the constant movement of carriages back and forth. The canal runs beneath the railway and passes the unlikely combination of a nightclub and refuse disposal plant.

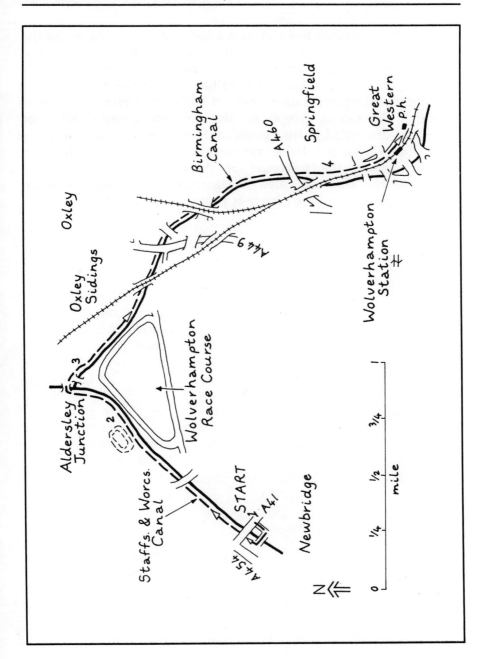

4. It rises up through locks to pass a lock keeper's cottage and the Broad Street Basin. Leave the towpath here to re-emerge into the world of traffic and noise, but only momentarily. Go left along Broad Street under the railway, cross the road and cut right along a path running behind Wolverhampton High Level station. This is an exceptional feature with beautiful Italianate arches and tiled walls, spoilt only by lack of care and by graffiti. Go right for the station but otherwise keep ahead to run through the forecourt of Wolverhampton Low Level station and through gates to Sun Street. The Great Western stands proudly on the corner opposite.

6. COMPTON

Route: Compton – Wightwick Bridge – Mops Farm Bridge – Kingswinford Branch Railway Walk – Compton

Distance: 4 miles

Map: O.S. Pathfinder Sheet 912 Wolverhampton (South)

Start: The Swan, Compton

Access: Compton is well served by buses from Wolverhampton. Travel on the A454 from Wolverhampton. Parking is limited.

The Swan, Holloway. Tel: (0902) 754736

The 300 year old Swan is a traditional Banks's hostelry with a number of rooms and a convivial atmosphere. The bar room is particularly old fashioned with its tiled floor and benches. It is the sort of place you hope will never change.

The Swan serves Banks's Mild and Bitter as well as Cameron's Strongarm. Rolls are available and families are welcome in the games room. There are benches outside near to the car park but no garden as such. Opening times are from 11am until 3pm and from 5pm in the evening on Mondays to Fridays. The Swan is open all day on Saturday and usual hours on Sunday. A very good local where the walker is always welcome.

Wightwick Manor

Just off the main Bridgnorth Road and a five-minute detour from the ramble is the half timbered Wightwick Manor, a Victorian masterpiece with several interesting features such as the impressive Great Parlour and unusually shaped Drawing Room. The manor features glass by Kempe and decoration by William Morris, two Victorian contemporaries who are renowned for their design and architectural comment. The manor is administered by the National Trust.

Wightwick Manor

The Walk

1. From The Swan turn left into the main road and follow it around to the right at the island. Go left down to the towpath at the bridge and then right on the path to walk beneath it. This very quickly leads out to the countryside.

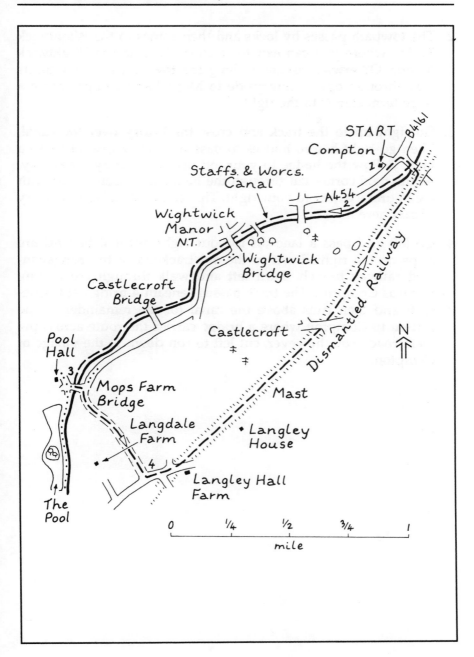

2. The towpath passes by locks and then comes to the Wightwick Bridge where you can exit for a short diversion to Wightwick Manor. Otherwise continue along the towpath as it winds its way through open countryside to Mops Farm Bridge where a large farm stands to the right.

3. Go right up to the track and cross the bridge over the canal. Then go right before houses to pass through a gateway into a field. Follow the hedge to your left up to a stile by a gateway. At the field corner cut through the hedge and keep ahead with the boundary now to your right. This exits onto a lane. Be wary of cars here.

4. Go left and pass a lane off to your right but just beyond are steps on the right down to the old trackbed of the Kingswinford railway branch. Turn left and walk through the cutting towards Compton. The track passes beneath a bridge at Castlecroft and then runs above the canal for the remainder of the section to Compton where a bridge carries the route across the main road. You, however, cut left to run down to the village of Compton.

7. THE DINGLE, WALSALL

Route: The Three Crowns — The Dingle — Cuckoo's Nook — Sutton Road — Three Crowns

Distance: 2 miles

Map: O.S. Pathfinder Sheet 913 Sutton Coldfield and Walsall

Start: The Three Crowns, Sutton Road

Access: There are regular buses along the Sutton Road from Walsall to Sutton Coldfield. Car drivers should head for the B4151 road to Sutton. There is parking near to The Three Crowns.

The Oak Inn, Walsall. Tel: (0922) 645758

The Oak Inn on Green Street, a five minutes walk from Walsall centre and railway station, is a wonderfully relaxing pub where a range of beers are served from a distinctive island bar. It offers Pitfield beers from Stourbridge as well as a rolling programme of guest brews.

Food is available at lunchtimes until 2pm and from 7 – 9pm in the evenings except Tuesday, Saturday and Sunday evenings. The pub is not really geared up for families but there is a beer garden. Opening hours at the Oak Inn are from noon until 2.30pm on Mondays to Fridays and 11.30 until 3pm on Saturdays. Evening opening is 7pm every night. The Oak is not open Sunday lunchtimes but does open Sunday evening from 7pm – 10.30pm.

For those who do not wish to travel into Walsall, the Three Crowns on the Sutton Road is a large M&B house with a large number of seats outside.

Walsall Leather Museum

Beacon Way

The walk joins the Beacon Way in The Dingle, a route through the borough of Walsall which features Barr Beacon, a summit where it is said that ancient Druids held sacrificial gatherings. This is the centre of a long thin strip of countryside known as Beacon Regional Park. Nearby is Hayhead Nature Trail near to the Rushall Canal. The trail features what was once the Hayhead Lime Works.

The Walk

1. Turn right from the entrance to the Three Crowns and right again along a path to cross a stile before joining a field's edge. Keep ahead to another stile and then proceed slightly right over the field. You will see Hayhead Farm to the left down a muddy lane.

2. You now cross the muddy track to enter a small wooded dingle and known as such locally, a place where wildlife thrives in and around the small pools and where the canopy of trees shades you during the warmer part of the day. There's a feeling that you are miles away from urbanisation. The path follows the dingle as it twists right and then continues to the top left corner of the wood where you join Beacons Way (which is waymarked). There are other paths and they should lead to the top far right corner of Cuckoo's Nook.

3. Cross a stile to exit the wood and keep ahead through the first field. Cross a stile and continue onwards, with Birch Wood to your left, to another stile. Once over maintain a similar route ahead to the Sutton Road.

4. To extend the walk it is possible to follow Beacons Way up to the high ground of Barr Beacon. The route is well waymarked. Otherwise it is a right turn here. There's a path on the other

side of the road but also a large verge on this side where you face the traffic. It is a short section before you join the old road, passing by a garage and garden centre before reaching The Three Crowns.

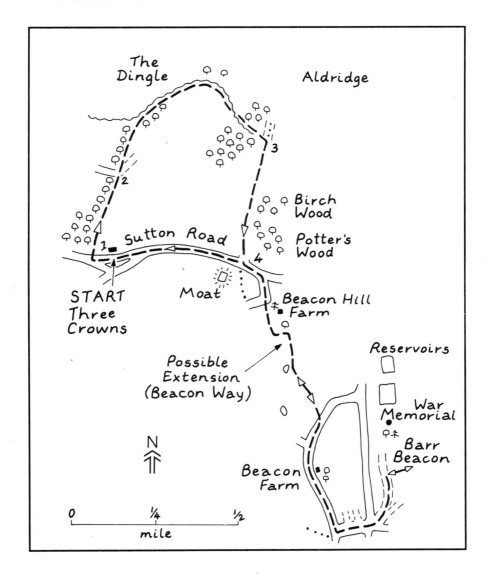

8. WEDNESBURY

Route: Leathern Bottel — Brunswick Park — River Tame — Tame Valley Canal — Crankhall Lane — Leathern Bottel

Distance: 3.5 miles

Map: O.S. Pathfinder sheets 912 Wolverhampton (South) and 913 Sutton Coldfield and Walsall

Start: The Leathern Bottel, Vicarage Road

Access: Wednesbury is well served by buses from Walsall and Wolverhampton. Wednesbury is signposted off the A41 from Wolverhampton. The one way system causes problems for those not certain of their directions. Head for Brunswick Park and then Vicarage Road.

The Leathern Bottel. Tel: 021 556 7214

This fascinating old pub is tucked away in a quiet corner of Wednesbury just outside the main centre. It has been a Mitchells and Butler house since the early 1900s although records suggest the original inn dates from the 16th century. It was, no doubt, a coaching inn between Walsall and Wednesbury. Some suggest that Dick Turpin might have set foot inside but the evidence to verify this is as scant here as elsewhere.

The traditional and cosy interior of this pub attracts folk from miles around. On handpull is Highgate Dark, Worthington and Bass. Food is served from noon until 2pm and from 6 until 8.30pm. Opening hours are from noon until 2.30pm and from 6pm in the evening on weekdays and usual hours on Sundays.

The Leathern Bottel, Wednesbury

Wednesbury

Described by one writer twenty years ago as "a town with some odd and ancient character", this hillside settlement looks over the Tame Valley. It has an illustrious industrial past dating from the 17th century when the famous Wednesbury Forge was established and gun making was of particular importance to the area. The town is now in transition and the Tame Valley has been the subject of considerable environmental improvement of which the walk takes advantage.

The Walk

1. From the Leathern Bottel, cross Vicarage Road into Clarkson Road and walk up to the busy thoroughfare of Wood Green Street. Cross over and enter Brunswick Park which exhibits fine wrought iron gates and a splendid clock to check the time against.

2. Pass to the right of the lodge and then turn left and then right to walk through the park, eventually passing to the right of a play area. On reaching the road cross over to proceed under the railway bridge to enter Crankhall Lane.

3. Turn right along Friar Street and ahead into Brookside, through a small industrial estate. This leads to a group of houses and a road. Go left here and then right to the River Tame. Turn right to follow the right bank of the River Tame up to Hydes Road.

4. Cross it and continue ahead into Woden Road, leaving the pavement to cut left to Hydes Pool, a wildlife area where you'll see Canada geese, great crested grebe, coot and moorhen. Return to the pavement to pass the college and then turn left into Bridge Street.

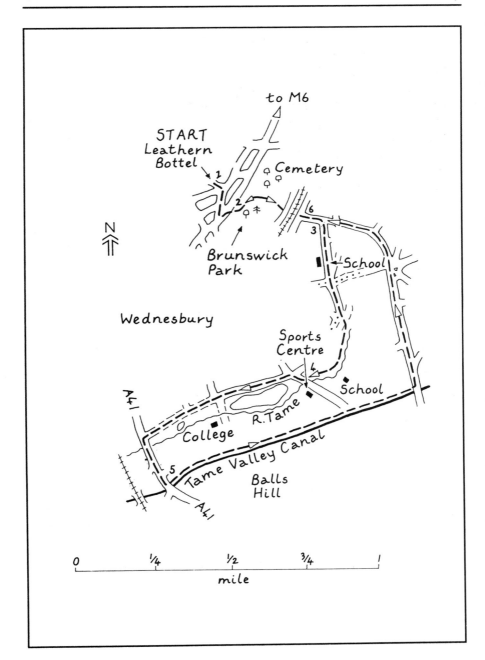

5. On reaching the bridge over the Tame Canal drop down to the towpath and turn left for a mile walk. This is a straight canal built to link the Rushall canal at Rushall Junction with the Walsall Canal at Tame Valley Junction. You leave the canal at Crankhall Lane Bridge up a set of steep steps climbing out of the cutting. Go left on Crankhall Lane. It is possible to follow this back to Brunswick Park. If you prefer quieter streets, turn left into Johnson Road and first right into Walton Road. Pass the school to reach Price Road and you can go straight ahead here to retrace your steps through the Tame Valley to Crankhall Lane. Otherwise turn right along William Green Road.

6. Either way, you need to retrace your steps under the railway bridge and up through Brunswick Park to return to the Leathern Bottel for a well-deserved spot of refreshment.

9. COSELEY

Route: Coseley Railway Station – Kenelm Road – Birmingham Canal – Tipton – Dudley Port Railway Station – Smethwick.

Distance: 6 miles (but a possibility of several shorter walks)

Map: O.S. Pathfinder sheet 912 Wolverhampton (South)

Start: Coseley Railway Station

Access: There is a good train service between Coseley and Smethwick Rolfe St which can be used to facilitate this linear ramble. You can shorten the walk by exiting the canal at Tipton, or Sandwell and Dudley railway stations. Coseley is signposted off the A4123 Birmingham New Road. There is parking near to the station.

The Painters Arms, Avenue Road, Coseley.
Tel: (0902) 883095

The narrow front of this old inn is deceiving, for step inside and the hostelry appears much larger. This does not diminish its friendliness for this is a traditional Holdens hostelry which serves the range of brews from the Woodsetton Brewery no more than a couple of miles away.

The Painters Arms is five minutes walk from Coseley railway station. Turn right into Fullwoods End. This rises to Tunnel Street and Avenue Road is on the left. It is worth a little detour to try a tipple before or after the ramble. The pub is open all day on weekdays and usual hours on Sundays. Food is available from noon until 2pm Mondays to Saturdays and from 7 – 9pm on Tuesday, Friday and Saturday evenings. Families are welcome and there is a patio outside where barbecues are held in the summer when the weather is good.

The Waggon and Horses, Church St, Oldbury.
Tel: 021 552 5467

This exceptional Victorian tiled pub with its original Holts brewery windows is a Grade II listed building. More surprisingly is that much of the bar is original too. It is something of a mecca for real ale drinkers for there are always at least 11 brews on at any given time including Adnams, Bathams, Everards and a rolling programme of guest beers.

The Waggon and Horses is renowned for its food too. This is available from noon until 2pm (1.30pm on Sundays) and from 6pm until 9pm in the evening although these finishing times might be half an hour later on Fridays and Saturday. The pub is open from 12 until 2.30 on weekdays (3pm on Fridays) and from 5pm in the evening (6pm on Saturdays). Sunday hours are from noon until 2.30pm and from 7pm until 10.30pm.

The Birmingham to Wolverhampton Main Line Canal, Coseley

Coseley

Coseley is one of the smaller Black Country towns which grew up with the boom in factories and foundries of the last century fuelled by local coal mining. Like so many Black Country towns Coseley runs into surrounding settlements for there are few distinctive boundaries in this compact urban territory.

Smethwick

The concentration of canals and railways at Smethwick reflects the importance of the area during the rapid growth era of the industrial revolution in the last century. There are a number of urban trails and walks based on the latter part of the walk including the splendid Galton Bridge constructed under the guidance of Thomas Telford in the late 1820s. The work of Brindley, Smeaton and Telford can been seen within this compact area where much restoration has taken place in recent times.

The Walk

(A torch would be useful)

1. Leave Coseley railway station and turn right into Fullwoods End, where there are shops on the right. Pass by these to turn right into Kenelm Road. This descends gently and at the end turn left along a track which leads to the Wolverhampton to Birmingham canal.

2. Turn left on the towpath which has been upgraded in recent years to accommodate cycles more readily than hitherto. The Birmingham and Black Country Canal cycleway is absolute bliss for cyclists seeking a traffic free route between the Black Country and Birmingham. There appears to be very little conflict with walkers too as there is usually plenty of room for all.

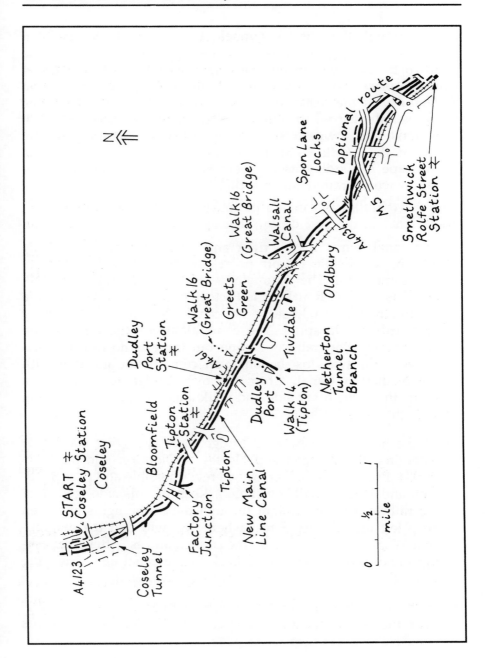

3. Go through the Coseley Tunnel. A torch would be useful if only to warn others walking in the opposite direction as the towpath narrows beneath the dripping walls of this Victorian masterpiece. You emerge only to the prospect of Beans Iron Foundry in the distance, a reminder of the magnitude of the industrial base which once nestled alongside these now still waters. The towpath soon brings you to Factory Junction, where the Dudley Canal branches off to pass beneath the hillscape of Dudley itself. There has been considerable restoration work around this junction which is pleasing to the eye as will be the Old Bush (Banks's) on your left if you are a touch thirsty.

4. The canal bends to the right and passes by Tipton railway station, a possible cut-off point for those in need of more refreshment for The Fountain is a mere two minutes walk away as is the O'Rourkes Pie Factory pub. Otherwise, continue ahead along a straight section of canal which is only broken by boatyards or old spurs. You come alongside the railway line and Dudley Port railway station but there is no direct access between the two. Just beyond you come to the junction with the Netherton Canal. Cross the over bridge to now join a footpath on the other side and walk ahead to pass the junction with the Walsall Canal.

5. At the next main new road bridge there is a good reason for emerging, the Waggon and Horses at Oldbury. Join the busy A4034, Bromford Road, cross wherever possible and pass Sandwell and Dudley Railway station. Keep on this side, go under the railway bridge, straight through the traffic lights and then keep left into Church Street where you will find the magnificent Waggon and Horses by the council offices. After a refreshing break retrace your steps back to the canal and rejoin the towpath to continue walking towards Birmingham.

6. You soon come to Bromford junction. Keep to the right here, over the footbridge to a towpath on the left and onwards

towards Smethwick. The canal is shadowed by the M5 motor-way and Spon Lane bridges. Go through Galton Tunnel and past Brass House Bridge. This passes under Engine Branch where you exit immediately at the next bridge.

7. Turn right at the road over the canal. At the junction with Rolfe Street turn right and Rolfe Street Station is approximately half a mile on the left.

10. SEDGLEY

Route: The Beacon Hotel — Bilston Street — Ettymore Road — Greenleighs — Sedgley Beacon — The Beacon Hotel

Distance: 2.5 miles

Map: O.S. Pathfinder Sheet 912 Wolverhampton (South)

Start: The Beacon Hotel, Sedgley

Access: Sedgley is served by regular buses from Dudley, Wolverhampton and elsewhere.

The Beacon Hotel, Sedgley. Tel: (0902) 883380

This beautifully restored public house is a joy to drink in. There are several rooms of differing character which are served from a central bar which looks as if it could be a confessional. After two pints of the exquisite Ruby Mild it might seem like it! The Victorian interior is surpassed only by a walk to the toilets through the conservatory which is as it should be, full of interesting plants which enjoy the warmth of the location.

To the rear stands the small Sarah Hughes Victorian brewhouse (dating from the 1850s) where an enthusiastic brewer not only produces the very palatable Ruby Mild and Sedgley Surprise, but will also illustrate the art of brewing on brewery open days. It evidently lay idle for 30 years until 1987 when its fortunes were revived. A 'phone call is necessary to confirm a booking. The brewery still maintains the name of Sarah Hughes on the wall and the entire venture is still in the hands of the Hughes family.

On handpull you'll find Sarah Hughes Ruby Mild (at an original gravity of 1058) and Sedgley Surprise. There's also M&B Mild, Hook Norton best bitter and another guest beer. There's a family room to the rear and a beer garden – so children are welcome at reasonable hours. There is usually no food available. The Beacon Hotel is open from noon until 2.30pm on Mondays to Fridays and from 5.30pm in the evening until 10.45pm. On Saturdays it is open from 11.30 until 3pm and from 6.00pm until 11pm. A splendid hostelry, an absolute must for the discerning drinker.

Sedgley

This is the high ground of the Black Country and the small central core of Sedgley still nestles around the 19th century Gothic parish church. It is also the easiest access point to Sedgley Beacon said to have been used to warn of invading armies throughout the ages. Sedgley has an industrial background. It is known that mining for shallow seams of coal took place in the 13th century and continued throughout the centuries. Sedgley became famous for its nail making and attracted hundreds of nailers who worked from small workshops attached to their dwellings.

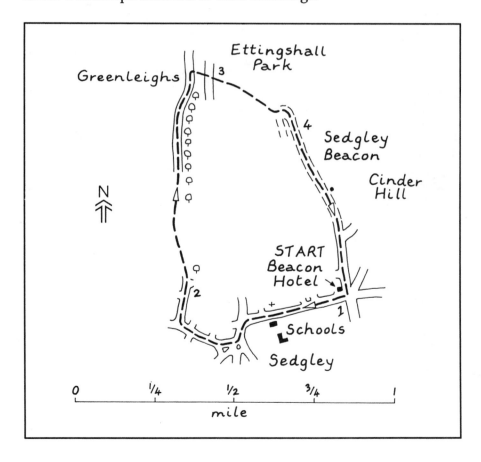

The Walk

1. Start from the entrance of the Beacon Hotel (there's a bus stop right outside). Turn right to walk up Bilston Street. Turn left and then at the centre cross over and go right along Ettymore Road. Descend to Hickemerlands Lane which branches off to the right. Go along it and find the old track which runs between two sections of road. This soon crosses the road and continues ahead.

2. The track bends right through woodland and straightens. Look for a stile on the right and then turn left to walk alongside a hedge between the path and lane. Cross a stile in the next boundary and pass by a farm. The path leads to a narrow track passing behind houses then opening up to a road in a very quiet residential area. Go right up a track known as Green-leighs and venture out onto the main Wolverhampton Road.

3. Cross the road and turn right. Walk on the rough road away from the hum of the traffic and then go left along a track signposted on the left through Springfield Farm. Walk through the farm buildings and the track continues to climb up the bank into an area of scrub land and through barriers. The path continues to climb up through rough grass to a junction. Go right and climb up to the summit. There is a way up on the left and through a gap in the fencing to reach the ridge. The views across the Midlands are impressive.

4. Walk along the crown of the ridge which soon dips. Continue ahead to rise up to the Beacon, now dominated by surrounding telecommunications towers. Walk up to the green gates and pass by the beacon along a track which becomes Beacon Lane. Return to the welcoming Beacon Hotel.

11. PENN COMMON

Route: Penn Church – Penn Common – Gospel End – Penn Church

Distance: 3 miles

Map: O.S. Pathfinder Sheet 912 Wolverhampton (South)

Start: Penn Church

Access: There are very frequent buses from Wolverhampton along the Penn Road to Church Hill but fewer turn left for Penn. Those travelling by car should follow the Penn Road (A449) until Church Hill. Turn left up to Penn church and there is car parking nearby on the right.

The Old Stag's Head. Tel: (0902) 341023

The Old Stag's Head has a number of pictures on the wall depicting great racing scenes of the past as one would imagine with the name of the house. This is a two-roomed pub with a lounge to the left and a smaller traditional bar to the right where the concerns of the world are put to right. The Old Stag's Head serves a very tasty pint of Banks's Mild and Bitter and offers food from noon until 2pm daily and from 6 – 9pm in the evening except Sunday. Opening times are from 11.30 until 3pm and from 6pm on Mondays to Fridays and all day Saturday. Usual Sunday hours prevail. There's a warm welcome at the Old Stag's Head.

Penn

It is claimed that the preaching cross, of which there are restored remains, was erected by Leofric and his wife, Lady Godiva of Coventry fame. The site is perfect with views over lower lying land to Gospel End and across to Shropshire. Penn church stands as a landmark throughout the walk.

Penn church

The Walk

1. Turn left out of the entrance to Penn Church into Pennwood Lane. This continues ahead at the junction but you go right into Sedgley Road. The Stag's Head stands on your left. Notice the old water trough. The road descends to Pennwood Common.

2. At the last houses go left along an unmade track. The path leaves a track before a gateway with a private notice to run along the hedge by the golf course towards the club house.

3. This follows the perimeter of the golf course to a track. Enter the car park beyond the club house and at the far end (before Pennwood Farm) turn right along a track through the trees. The track more or less follows the left boundary of the golf course and can get muddy.

4. It descends almost to the Penn Brook but beforehand go right, not immediately right onto the course, but ahead towards a house. Pass the house and join a track but before the next house go left to go over a stile.

5. This leads down to the brook, cross the footbridge and head slightly left up the bank. Cross a stile and walk ahead. You can see the Baggeridge Brick works on the horizon. Cross the next stile and keep ahead to another stile. Once over head for a gap between houses. You exit onto the main road in Gospel End. The Summerhouse is to the left if you wish to take refreshment.

6. Otherwise go right along the pavement. Cross the triangular junction of Penn Road and look for a stile on the right by a gate, opposite the entrance to Baggeridge Country Park. Follow the field's edge into the valley. At the bottom go left and follow the line of hawthorns to a gate. Go through it and keep ahead to cross a stile. Continue ahead to cross another two stiles and then head down to the stream.

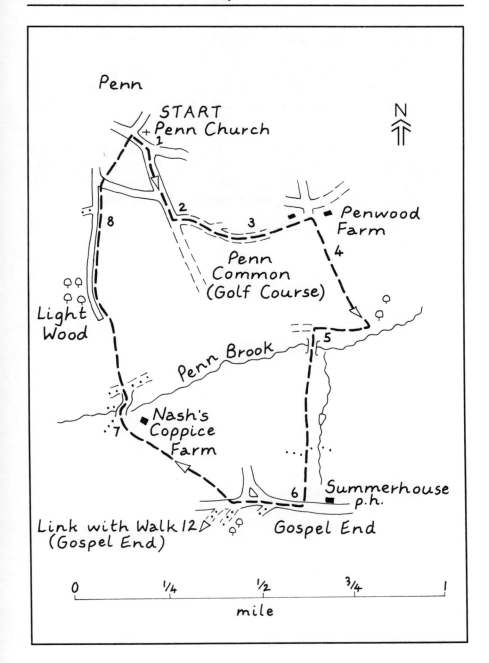

7. Cross the footbridge and walk slightly right through an enclosure to cross a stile by a gate. The path leads to a road. Cross it and join a track on the golf course which runs to the left at first. It then curves right up to woodland and crosses a track. The track now keeps company with a hedge on the left-hand side.

8. The track comes to a junction and bridleway which continues ahead. Cross the stile next to it and follow the hedge alongside the old track. You come to a final field before Penn church where you bear right diagonally right across the field.

12. GOSPEL END

Route: Gospel End — Baggeridge Country Park — Himley Hall — Wombourne — Gospel End

Distance: 6 miles

Map: O.S. Pathfinder Sheet 912 Wolverhampton (South)

Start: The Summerhouse, Gospel End

Access: There is a bus service from Dudley to Gospel End. Travel on the A463 road. There is parking at Baggeridge country park.

The Summerhouse. Tel: (0902) 676102

The Summerhouse is set back from the main road, an attractive looking hostelry which is several hundred years old. The pub is larger than it looks at first glance and is very popular on warm summer days as there is a large garden area with plenty of amusements for children.

Banks's Bitter and Mild is served as is Hanson's Mild. Food is served from noon until 2pm every day and from 6pm until 9pm in the evening on weekdays. Families are welcome indoors if eating as there is an area away from the bar. The Summerhouse is open from noon until 3pm daily and from 6pm in the evenings. Usual Sunday hours prevail.

Baggeridge Country Park

This country park, established next to the Baggeridge Brick Works, is a good example of restoration of a landscape from previous workings. There is a visitor centre and a number of short walks throughout the park.

The Middle Pool, Baggeridge Country Park.

The park leads down to Himley Hall, previously the home of the Earls of Dudley. Built in the 1820s by William Atkinson, the hall supersedes earlier buildings. The landscaped gardens are kept well and are a joy to walk at any time of the year.

The Walk

1. Turn right from the Summerhouse and pass the two roads on the right which run through to Penn Common before crossing to the entrance of Baggeridge Country Park on the left. Walk along the verge along the narrow road which leads to the visitor centre. There are opportunities to cut the road corners but stay near to it.

2. Walk through the car park to the left of the visitor centre buildings to enter a grass amphitheatre. This leads to an

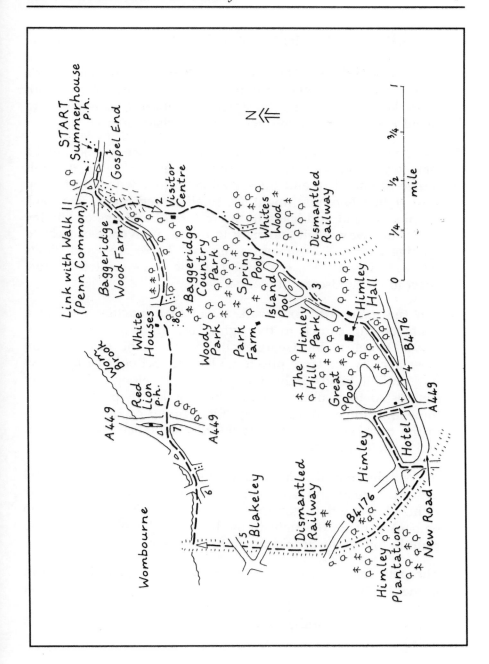

aggregate path. Go right here and walk down to a junction. Bear left over a footbridge and you will see Spring and Island Pools to your right. There are little diversions to the water's edge if you wish. Otherwise keep left at the turnings for both pools, keeping ahead by the stream (waymarked in red) and to Island Pool which is often frequented by fishermen.

3. The path runs alongside the pool and crosses a stile onto a main track. Go left and walk into Himley Park with the golf course to your left, and Rock Pool beneath a wooded bluff on your right where you might see small carved caves. The track becomes a road and leads to the restored buildings of Himley Hall. Your way is left and right to follow an avenue of trees to a lodge gate and a miniature railway. There are good views across to Great Pool, the largest of the lakes created to give effect to the landscape. It works.

4. Join the main road and walk ahead to a junction passing a plain looking church to the right. Turn right to pass Himley House Hotel, a fine Georgian building. At the next junction cross over by the large pub to go left into School Road. Follow this until it bends right, but you go left along a bridleway signposted to Wallheath. Cross the Himley by-pass and continue ahead to a railway bridge. Once under go right to rise up to the trackbed of the Kingswinford old branch track. Go left and walk into Wombourne.

5. In Wombourne the track goes under a corrugated tunnel beneath a road and you will soon see a playground on your right. This is where you exit by taking a little path down the embankment on the right to the banks of the Wom Brook. Go right to follow the brookside up to the village.

6. The path reaches a road. Go right into Gravel Hill but almost immediately turn left into Rookery Road. Part way up bear right into a narrow back road, Battlefield Lane which brings you to the Stourbridge Road. On the left down the old road

section is the Red Lion (see Wombourne walk) which is well worth a diversion for a break.

7. Otherwise put on a brave face, grit your teeth and wait for a lull in the traffic to cross this horrendous road. On the other side is the haven. Walk through a kissing gate and proceed up a track. Proceed through the kissing gate by a house and then follow the well walked path which leads up the Baggeridge Wood.

8. Cross a stile by a wall and pass by the ruins of the now forlorn ruins of White Houses. Continue onward through the wood to enter a pocket of a field. Keep ahead and re-enter the wood. There are great views along this section of South Staffordshire and across to Shropshire's favourite hill, the Wrekin or south to The Malverns.

9. The path comes alongside the farm buildings of Baggeridge Wood Farm. Cross a stile to the right of them and enter a small path into the wood. This leads to a track where you turn left and left again for Gospel End or right for the country park visitor centre.

13. WOMBOURNE

Route: The Bratch – Awbridge Bridge – Railway – The Bratch

Distance: 3 miles

Map: O.S. Pathfinder 912 Wolverhampton (South)

Start: Wombourne Old Railway Station (or bus travellers from the stops in Bullmeadow Lane)

Access: There are regular buses from Wolverhampton, Dudley and Stourbridge to Wombourne. Alight at Bullmeadow Lane and walk down Bratch Lane. This is where car users will want to park at the old railway station. Wombourne is situated off the A449.

The Red Lion. Tel: (0902) 892270

The Red Lion is a busy pub with a regular locals trade. It has a lounge area on the right given over much to eating and a bar to the left of the pretty front door. The Red Lion has always been a country roadside pub dating back to 1810. There's a selection of beers on the pump including Banks's Mild, Worthington Bitter, Bass and Marston's Pedigree.

Food is available at lunch and evenings except Sunday evening. Families are welcome and there is a garden and outdoor area. The Red Lion is open from 11.30am until 11pm weekdays and usual hours on Sundays. Call into this cheerful pub for a break.

When in Wombourne you might also consider The Old Bush on High Street, a pub which offers Banks's Mild and Bitter in congenial surroundings.

Wombourne

The village is nestled around a well preserved green and church dedicated unusually to St Benedict Biscop. The village is well-known for its quaint centre, but more for the ornate Bratch locks and toll house on the Staffordshire and Worcestershire Canal. This navigation exhibits some of the finest work of James Brindley; it is a very rural canal in character and one which is becoming increasingly popular with boaters. Nearby stands the handsome brick building belonging to the local waterworks. Altogether, these architectural delights make the walk so enjoyable.

Bratch Locks

The ramble also features the Kingswinford Railway Walk, an important recreational network throughout the area. The old station at Wombourne is well preserved and houses the ranger service and a cafe. It only had a working life of about 40 years before closure.

Once, the aim of the railway had been to branch out to Bridgnorth, but the GWR were very tardy in supporting the proposals. The then Earl of Dudley dampened their aspirations for good when he pushed for a direct passenger link between Stourbridge Junction and Wolverhampton. It seems like an eminently sensible idea when one considers the nature of the journey via Birmingham these days.

Considering that the railway came very late in the day (1910s) the route was engineered mainly by a work force of two hundred navvies who hand dug much of the works. The line was not fully open until 1924 and, in 1925, a steam-powered rail-car set off in a most optimistic fashion. It was closed in 1965 and dismantled a few years afterwards.

The Walk

1. From the old railway station return to Bratch Lane and turn right. The lane is narrow so keep an eye on the passing traffic. Notice on the left the ornate waterworks belonging to the South Staffordshire Water Company.

2. Turn right to join the towpath by Bratch Locks. The path crosses by the lock keepers cottage. It soon leaves houses behind to run through level countryside for a little less than a mile. Leave the towpath at Awbridge Bridge. Walk beneath the bridge then turn right up to the road.

3. Turn left to walk along a lane. At the fork go right into Flash

Lane. This soon reaches the overbridge of the railway track. Go beyond the bridge and then cut back left up to the trackbed. Then turn left to return to Wombourne railway station.

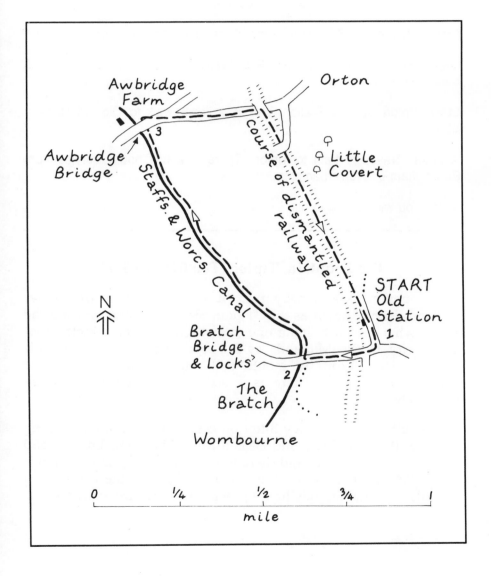

14. TIPTON

Route: Tipton – Netherton Tunnel – Cobbs Engine House – Darby End & Netherton(Diversion) – Garratt's Lane – Old Hill

Distance: 6 miles (8 miles if including the diversion)

Map: O.S. Pathfinder Sheets 912 Wolverhampton (South) and 933 Stourbridge

Start: Tipton Railway Station. This is a linear walk to Old Hill Railway Station

Access: Travel by train to Tipton. There is a half hourly service from Birmingham or Wolverhampton.

Note: You will need a torch!

The Fountain, Tipton. Tel: 021 520 8777

The Fountain is a homely pub. It is where the prize fighter William Perry, known as the "Tipton Slasher" trained during the 1850s; what sort of training one cannot tell. He was something of a celebrity in the Midlands as for seven years he retained his championship. Word of mouth still refers to the pub as The Slasher to this day. There is a statue in Tipton which commemorates the fighter.

The Fountain offers Tetley Bitter on cask but the more discerning seek out the Holt, Plant and Deakin Mild, Bitter and Entire. Food is served at lunchtimes and there is a beer garden. The Fountain is open from noon until 4.30pm and from 7pm in the evening on weekdays. Usual Sunday hours prevail. Families are welcome.

The Old Swan, Halesowen Road, Netherton.
Tel: (0384) 253075

The pub prospered for decades under the stewardship of a dear landlady known as Ma Pardoe; it was a Black Country institution. Unfortunately, since her death the pub cum brewery has seen mixed fortunes and at present is not brewing. Nevertheless, walkers should not by-pass this very old hostelry exhibiting a magnificent enamel ceiling and original bar which is virtually unique. Cask conditioned beers are from the Chainmaker beer company in Stourbridge.

The White Swan, Baptist End Road. Tel: (0384) 256101

Five minutes walk from the Old Swan is The White Swan (stay on the right and turn right into Baptist End Road), another former brew house from the last century. The landlord says there's a ghost in the bar, an old lady who lived at the pub during Edwardian times but she is very polite!

The White Swan is a very lively pub which welcomes walkers. On handpull is Banks's Mild and Bitter, Marston's Pedigree and the guest beer is usually Enville from South Staffordshire.

Food is available from noon until 2.30pm and from 6.30 to 8.30pm except Sunday evening. Opening times are from noon until 3pm and from 7pm in the evening on Mondays to Fridays and all day on Saturdays. Families are welcome and there is a large garden area with a children's area as well as a family room. You can be assured of a welcome here.

There's also the opportunity to call into the Dry Dock Inn at Windmill End, where there is a narrow boat in the bar!

Tipton

Unlike Dudley, Tipton grew up in the 19th century as a ragged industrial settlement with mines and works, spoil heaps and the social squalor related to such exploitation. It is certain that one of the earliest, if not the first commercially built, Newcomen engine was used here at Lady Meadow to pump water from the mine. Ironically, this engine or far more sophisticated pumping arrangements could save these pits from continual flooding and eventual abandonment. But Tipton would not be forgotten as a coal mining centre. One single block of coal weighing six tons, extracted from a Tipton mine, was exhibited at the world famous Crystal Palace Exhibition in 1851.

The canals were, however, the catalyst which made Tipton so important as a centre during the industrial boom of the mid-1900s. It seems fitting that this canal exploration begins here.

Netherton Tunnel

The Netherton Tunnel

The tunnel was completed as late as 1859 in an attempt to provide a less congested route through the Black Country than the Dudley Tunnel. At 3027 yards it is fairly lengthy and the towpath used to be lit at one time, firstly by gas lamps and then electricity generated by a nearby turbine house. There is no lighting now so a torch is an absolute must.

The southern end of the tunnel gives out at Windmill End junction where the ruins of Cobb's Engine House remain on the hillside. This housed an engine which pumped water from nearby mines into the canal.

The Walk

1. From Tipton station turn right to join the canal towpath on the left-hand side of Owen Street. Keep ahead to walk along the towpath of the Birmingham Main Line canal until you reach the junction with the Netherton Branch signposted to Hawne Basin.

2. Go over the footbridge and continue along the towpath until the portals of this magnificent tunnel. Torch on and through you go. It is approximately one mile in length so prepare for at least twenty minutes of darkness.

3. You emerge into daylight once more to see Cobb's Engine House on the left. Before Windmill End junction go left over the footbridge and then ahead over the Hawne Basin branch. Go left if continuing at this stage to follow it.

4. However, those who wish to divert in search of refreshment should continue along the towpath to pass the one-time junction of the delightfully named Bumblehole Branch. This passes beneath a road bridge. At the second exit join Northfield Road. You need to go right to climb up to Netherton. You will reach

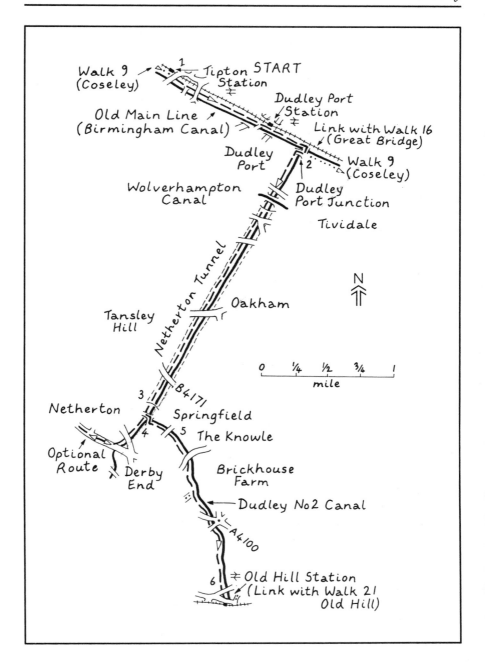

the main Halesowen Road. Go right and second right into Baptist End Road for The White Swan or left for the Old Swan which is on the Halesowen Road. After being suitably refreshed make your way back to the Windmill End junction. This is not forgetting that there is an enterprising inn by the canal here, The Dry Dock with its very own narrow boat in the bar. A little contrived for some but nevertheless a most interesting hostelry which serves real ale and offers food.

5. Now head for Hawne Basin along a quiet canal which has attracted wildlife and unfortunately litter and rubbish too. This does not detract from its naturalness with encroaching banks providing shelter for coots, ducks and swans. You pass under a main bridge below Garratt's Lane and then it is a matter of half a mile to Waterfall lane Bridge.

6. Turn right for Old Hill Station which is just to the left at the first main junction.

15. WOODSETTON

Route: Park Inn – Wren's Nest Hill – Wrens Hill Road – Park Inn

Distance: 2.5 miles

Map: O.S.Pathfinder sheet 912 Wolverhampton (South)

Start: Park Inn, Woodsetton

Access: Woodsetton has a regular bus service. Those travelling by car should come off the Birmingham New Road into Sedgley Road.

The Park Inn. Tel: (0902) 882843

The Park Inn is the brewery tap of Holden's brewery which stands alongside. It is a large pub centred around a square bar and with a separate conservatory area and an outdoor area so is well used by families at lunchtimes. The Park Inn is also a busy but friendly pub which sells the Holden's range of brews.

Food is available at lunchtimes until 2.15pm and from 6pm until 9pm and on several nights there is a barbecue (usually at weekends). The brewery tap is open all day throughout the week and usual hours on Sundays.

Wren's Nest National Nature Reserve

This famous geological site is estimated to be 42 million years old. It is known internationally for its geological structures and is a mecca for fossil hunters who are being urged not to take any more of the fine specimens of trilobites (known as the Dudley Bug). People are genuinely asked to leave their fossil hammers at home! A selection of fossils can be seen at the Dudley Museum.

This outcrop of Wenlock limestone has been quarried in previous ages and there are also a number of natural caverns to be found. There is a leaflet to explain the flowers and woodlands of the reserve.

The Walk

1. Turn right from the Park Inn and turn right again as you enter Dawlish Road. Follow the track to pass by a farm and then a cottage on the left. At the junction go left and follow the path through woodland and old workings, up steps and down more than once before coming to an old quarry working on the right. Go right through the gateway and then cross Wrens Hill Road.

2. The path continues ahead, running behind houses. It is a tranquil part and spoilt only by inconsiderate dog fouling. As the path sweeps left continue onward and cross another path. You come alongside wooden fencing where you go right on the next main track reached. You have gone too far if you begin to approach a children's play area.

3. Cross the main route (Waymarked number 7) and climb up

steps. The path begins to curve right and then continues ahead in a winding fashion. The path curves right again towards the rock faces then rises again, keeping ahead to Wrens Hill Road. You can divert right to see the caves and extractions if you wish. Make sure you turn left eventually to exit by The Caves public house.

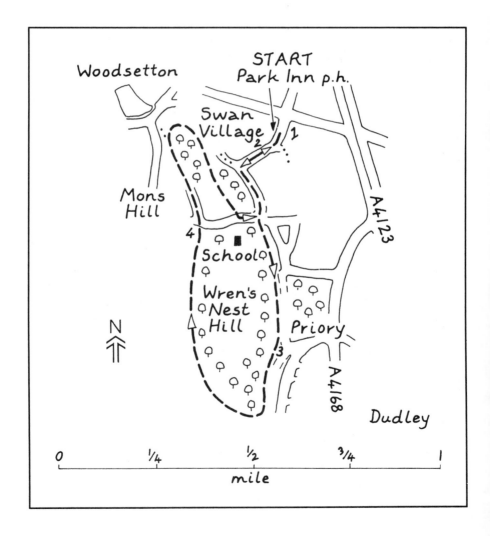

4. Whichever route you choose cross the Wrens Hill Road beneath the pub and follow the path as it descends. You reach a junction where you go right and the path curves right. At the next junction you have a choice of route. Those seeking a low level walk should go left, and then right to return to the cottage where you first joined the path. Those seeking high level adventure should bear right and climb up the side of Wren's Nest Hill. This eventually drops down to the road again where you go left to regain your steps back to the starting point.

16. GREAT BRIDGE

Route: Great Bridge – Wolverhampton to Birmingham Canal – Walsall Canal – Ryders Green Locks – Great Bridge

Distance: 4 miles

Map: O.S. Pathfinder Sheet 912 Wolverhampton (South)

Start: Market Place, Great Bridge (between Horseley Heath and Great Bridge roads)

Access: There are regular buses to Great Bridge and the nearest railway station is Dudley Port, a good 10 minutes walk from the centre of Great Bridge.

Great Bridge is at the intersection of the A461 and A4035. There is car parking in the town centre.

The Port 'n' Ale, 178 Horseley Heath. Tel: 021 557 7249

A very welcoming pub with a large lounge on the left and a cosier bar to the right. The pub is closer to Dudley Port Station than Great Bridge centre but is well worth the walk.

It has a range of beers including Bathams and, when the author called, an unusual brew for these parts – Freeminer from the Forest of Dean. There are usually several guest beers on tap at any one time.

The Port 'n' Ale is open from noon until 2.30pm and from 5.00pm in the evening on weekdays and usual Sunday times. Meals at lunchtimes only. When in Great Bridge you might also like to try the Royal Oak in Whitehall Road (B4166) which offers a range of guest beers and good food.

Eight Locks, Great Bridge

Great Bridge

Spoilt very much by road building the centre of Great Bridge provides a shopping centre for the locality. The walk features reclaimed land, now known as Sheepwash Urban Park, which now offers a haven for wildlife and a breath of fresh air from the surrounding urban areas.

Nearby Dudley Port was a creation of the industrial era, a busy zone where transhipment of goods became very important, hence the name. There were one or two breaches of canals hereabouts, the major disaster being the breach of 1899 when the clay-pit of the Rattlechain and Stour Valley Brickworks was flooded and several boats lost.

The Walsall canal offers an insight into what many of the canals would have been like earlier in the century where works are packed tight together, with wharves and cranes to despatch goods onto waiting narrow boats. There's a haunting sadness now as you step along this quiet corridor almost as an intruder disturbing the stillness. At Ryders Green you keep to the left at the junction to descend the impressive eight locks before Great Bridge.

The Walk

1. From the Market Place walk into Great Bridge Road on the right-hand pavement. Cut down right by billboards (although at some stage this might be developed) to walk alongside the remnants of a branch canal. This leads to Tame Road. Cross it and pass the Seven Stars public house and then go left down another path into a reclaimed works area which is now a series of pools which attracts all manner of birds.

2. The tracks heads towards the railway but then curves right to a small bridge over a stream. Once over cut left to follow the track under the railway. It then curves left up to a gap by a

gate leading to the towpath of the Wolverhampton to Birmingham Main Line canal.

3. Go right here and walk alongside this wider navigation. Pass by Brades Hall junction and keep ahead until you reach a main overbridge, Albion Bridge. Cross to the other side of the towpath and regain a path to Pudding Green Junction where the Walsall Canal begins. Go left to follow the towpath along this backwater passing all manner of works many of which owe their existence to the canal but no longer cherish its existence.

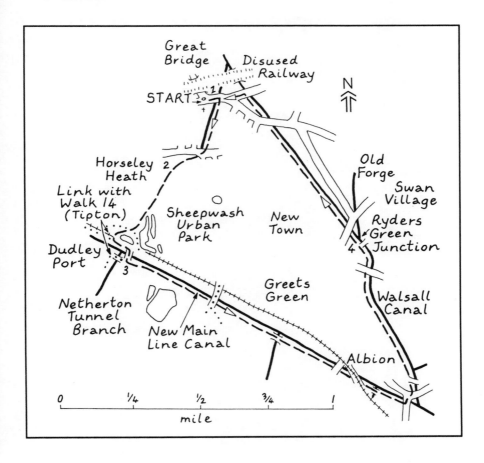

4. Pass by the remains of the Greets Green Basins and then arrive at Ryders Green Junction. Keep ahead as the Black Lake branch forks right. The flight of locks leads into Great Bridge under Great Bridge Street and then by a store car park. Look out for an exit at the next bridge, which is Brickhouse Lane. Go left up to the lane and then turn right to the Market Place.

17. WEST BROMWICH

Route: Sandwell Country Park – Swan Pool – Benedictine Priory – Sandwell Country Park

Distance: 2 miles

Map: O.S. Pathfinder Map 913 Sutton Coldfield and Walsall

Start: Sandwell Country Park car park

Access: Travel by bus to West Bromwich and then walk along Reform St into Lloyd's Dagger Lane. From West Bromwich (off the A41 Expressway) you require Lloyd's Dagger Lane then turn right onto Salter's Lane and right again for the access to the country park.

Churchfield Tavern, Little Lane.

This lively multi-roomed public house is one of the nearest public houses to Sandwell Country Park. You will have to retrace your steps back to Lloyd Daggers Lane, then cross directly into Kinniths's Way. Turn next right along Hallam Street and Little Lane is on the left by the hospital. It is a good 15 minute walk but well worth it.

The Churchfield serves Banks's Mild and Bitter in excellent condition. There is a small bar, as well as other rooms and a garden to the rear with a play area and animals which the children love. The pub is open from 11am until 11pm on weekdays and usual hours on Sunday.

Sandwell Country Park

Situated in Sandwell Country Park is the Sandwell Park Farm, a restored Queen Anne farm which is now a visitor and interpretive centre as well as a working farm. There are Victorian kitchen gardens and tea rooms here. A small admission charge is made to see the farm.

Sandwell Park Farm

The park really is an oasis amid noisy roads and miles of housing. It belonged originally to the Earls of Dartmouth, landed gentry who resided in Sandwell Hall which was demolished earlier in this century. On the walk you will come across the ruins of a Benedictine priory, founded in the late 12th century and sacked in the times of the dissolution of the monasteries. It is said that much of the raw material was used to build Sandwell Hall mentioned above.

This parkland survived the onslaught of urban development as West Bromwich grew very rapidly in the last century with dozens of works making iron artefacts ranging from stoves and grates, bedsteads and coffee-mills. This growth was chronicled in Pigot's *New Commercial Directory* of 1829:

"Only a few years ago, the portion of the parish where is situated the principal part of the village, was but a heath, in which rabbits burrowed . . . such a place is not now to be recognised; the inhabitants of men and establishments of artisans, have sprung up with surprising rapidity: and, from a place insignificant in its origin, West Bromwich has become important in its trade and manufactures, with a population enterprising and respectable."

Near to West Bromwich, however, are two fine timber framed buildings dating from earlier times, The Oak House dating from the 16th and 17th century, and The Manor House from medieval times. John Wesley preached a sermon to an exceedingly large gathering at the Oak House in 1774. Methodism was strong in the area and nearby at Great Barr is Astbury's Cottage, the home of Francis Astbury who became the first American Methodist bishop.

The Walk

1. From the bottom-right corner of the car park turn right, as signposted to Swan Pool and Nature Centre. This little path leads to a main track. Go left.

2. The track rises over the motorway bridge and then descends to woodland. Ignore the turning to your left. Keep ahead. On the left are the remains of a Benedictine priory. Follow the track up to the road but just before go left along another well-worn track.

3. This meets another track at a junction. You turn left here to walk down to Swan's Pool on your right. At the crossroads it is worth diverting right to walk alongside the lake as birds can

often be seen at close quarters. There's also the entertainment
of watching windsurfers challenging the wind.

4. Cross the motorway bridge and descend to parkland again.
You can choose your way back across the park taking any left
turn towards the Sandwell Farm Park and the car park.

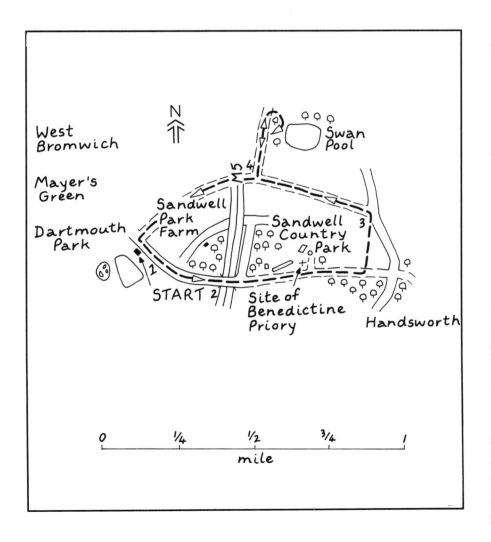

18. LOWER GORNAL

Route: Lower Gornal – Stickley Lane – The Dingle – Cotwall End – The Straits – Lower Gornal

Distance: 3 miles

Map: O.S. Pathfinder Sheet 912 Wolverhampton (South)

Start: The Miners Arms, Lower Gornal

Access: There are several buses to Fiveways, just one minute from the Miners Arms.

The Miners' Arms Lower Gornal. Tel: (0902) 882238

The Miners' Arms is a welcoming one-roomed local dating from 1835. It serves Holden's Black Country Bitter and Holden's Mild on handpull. The pub is also referred as the Old Chapel as once it was used for religious meetings by the Gornal Ranters. What looks like part of the old chapel buildings can be seen to the rear of the pub. Originally an old brew house, the pub was named the Miners Arms in 1887.

The Miners Arms is open from 2.30pm onwards on Mondays to Fridays and from noon until 4.30pm and from 7pm on Saturdays. It is open usual Sunday hours. Food is generally not available and there is no outside drinking area at the Miners.

Just up the road on the left-hand side stands another traditional pub, The Waggon and Horses. This was until recent times a Mild only pub reflecting the importance of Mild in this part of the Midlands. Ruiton Street offers even more choice with the Cross Keys nearby!

The Dingle, Lower Wood

Cotwall End Countryside and Craft Centre

Situated in Cotwall End Valley the centre amounts to 12 acres of grassland where animals and waterfowl roam – bantams, ducks, pigs and goats. It is also possible to see birds of prey, the owl, falcons and hawks.

Based at the centre are crafts people such as the maker of rocking horses in the Rocking Horse Stable, ceramics, wooden crafts, paintings and prints. It is a lovely place to call into midway on the ramble.

The Walk

1. From the entrance of the Miners Arms go right to climb Ruiton Street. Go left into Stickley Lane and then right towards Ellowes Hall School entrance. However, go right before the school gates along a fenced path which runs between gardens and the school grounds.

2. This eventually comes to a junction by a pool. Turn left down here to run alongside the playing fields. Ignore the first turning right but further down as the path bends to the left, go right down steps into a dingle, where you can walk through remnants of ancient woodland, see kingfishers darting along the waters and butterflies bobbing to and fro in the nearby meadows. It is a pleasant interlude from the surrounding built up areas.

3. Go over the bridge and come to a junction. Go left and then immediately right down steps and along the dingle. The path then rises up steps and by a field to exit at a car park at Cotwall End. Go through the car parking area and turn right on Cotwall End road.

4. At the corner go left along a track which passes through old farm buildings. The track continues ahead and runs alongside a

golf course. Keep to the rough ground and as you approach houses at The Straits a path cuts down to a green fence by a school behind gardens. It exits onto a road in a housing estate. Go left and left at the end of the road. Follow Longfellow Road down to Cotwall End Road.

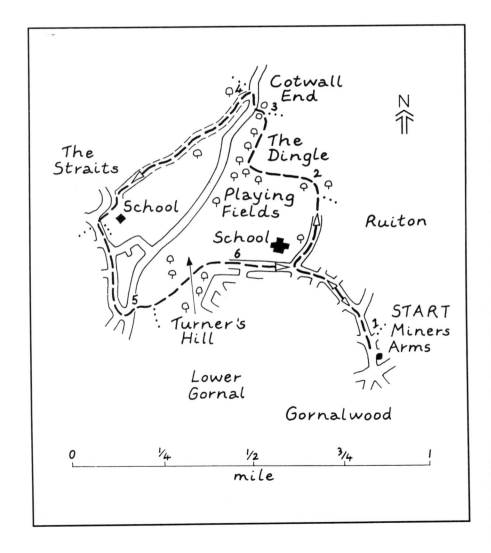

5. Go left for less than a hundred metres, cross the road and cross a stile into an area of scrub. Follow the path ahead, ignoring any turnings to the right. At the main junction go left beneath Turner's Hill wood. Climb up the valley and at the next junction bear right to climb up the hillside to a kissing gate. Go right here to houses.

5. Retrace your steps along Stickley Lane to Ruiton Street where you turn right to walk back to The Miners and Five Ways where the main bus stops are.

19. KINGSWINFORD

Route: Kingswinford Cross — Kingswinford church — Crooked House — Gornalwood

Distance: 4 miles

Map: O.S. Pathfinder Sheets 912 Wolverhampton (South) and 933 Stourbridge

Start: The crossroads in Kingswinford centre — Summer Hill, High Street, Moss Grove and Market Street

Access: There are regular buses from Dudley, Stourbridge and Wolverhampton. This is a linear walk between Kingswinford and Gornalwood. There are regular buses between the two places allowing a return to your start point if necessary.

The Crooked House. Tel: (0384) 238583

This is Himley's response to Pisa, for Crooked House leans as much as its name suggests. It is at first quite uncanny for without one sip of the nectar you feel slightly disorientated, curtains not hanging quite right, objects amiss. The explanation is that the area has been mined so much that the pub, which was originally known as the Glynne Arms, has been affected by subsidence.

In recent years the Crooked House has been re- furbished and an extension added to the rear. Banks's Mild and Bitter are on tap as is Marston's Pedigree. Food is served daily at lunch from noon until 2pm and evening meals from 6.30pm until 8.30pm but not Sunday. Children are welcome during meal times only and there are plenty of seats outside in this countryside spot. The Crooked House is open all day in the summer (from April until September) and from 11.30am until 2.30pm, and from 6.30pm again in the Winter (October to March). Usual Sunday hours prevail.

The Crooked House

Kingswinford.

This was described by a nineteenth century writer as a place full of "elegant villas" belonging to "capitalists of the glass trade" reflecting the important wealth creation for some of the glass business of Stourbridge. But much of the area was mined including the land surrounding the pretty little church of Kingswinford where many of the entrepreneurs of glass manufacture are buried. The ramble passes by here. There were also ironworks in the vicinity.

Kingswinford still retains a tradition of glassmaking and the Broadfield House Glass Museum contains a fine collection of glass from Roman times to the 20th century. The main displays are on colour, decorated and cut glass.

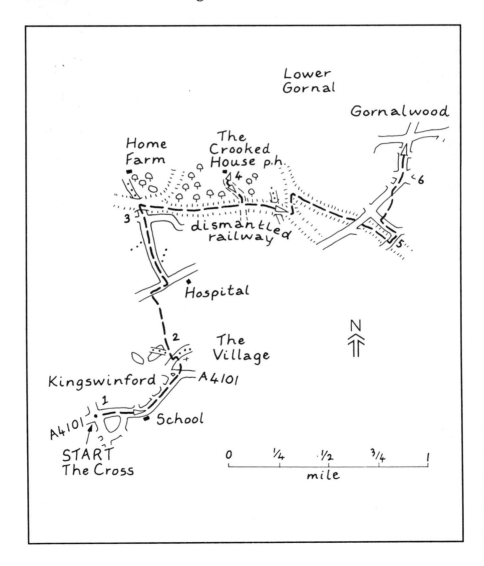

The Walk

1. This is a linear walk which begins at the main crossroads (known as the Cross) in Kingswinford. Turn left into High Street and walk along this main road for just under half a mile, passing the M.E.B. offices. Then go left by a little green, known as Park Lane. Go ahead to walk by the bowling green and along a path on the right towards Kingswinford church. Go next left towards the pool and pass by a school.

2. The path leads between houses and you then cross a road to walk along Pinewood Walk. Go left and right, then keep ahead to join Stallings Lane, opposite a supermarket. Turn right and then next left into Ham Lane. This rises through an industrial estate and at the corner go left into Holbeache Lane and immediately right along a track where a sign indicates "No Tipping".

3. Go under the railway bridge and then bear left to climb up to the old trackbed and countryside. Go left along the trackbed for about a quarter of a mile. You will see the pylons and be vigilant as you cross a little bridge over a track beneath. Cut down steps on the left here to join this track and go right down to the Crooked House.

4. Fully refreshed return to the old trackbed. Follow this as it curves gently right but then keep left as it descends. Then climb up, and follow the rail track which bears right, and straightens. This route, now the Pensnett Railway Walk, runs beneath Cinder Road, and then you soon come to a footbridge over the old railway.

5. Go left here up steps to the bridge. Turn left and walk up to pass a pub called The Forge on Chase Road. This modern pub has been rebuilt on the site of an old forge. Go left to pass the cemetery. After here, go right into open ground. Head for the top left corner where a little link path runs up to Cinder Road.

Go right for Gornalwood. Those seeking a bus back to Kingswinford will find a stop on the right (Bus 257).

6. Otherwise keep ahead at the crossroads and walk up Bull Street into the shopping area of Gornalwood.

20. BRIERLEY HILL

Route: The Vine – Delph Locks – Merry Hill – Pensnett Canal – Grove Pool – Stourbridge Canal Junction – Delph Locks – The Vine

Distance: 6 miles

Map: O.S. Pathfinder Sheet 933 Stourbridge

Start: The Vine, Delph Road

Access: Delph Road is off Mount Pleasant Road, a feeder road from the A4036 Pedmore Road. Most signs indicate the way to the nearby Merry Hill shopping centre. There are regular buses along Mill Street and Amblecote Road which pass the top of Delph Road.

The Vine (Bull and Bladder). Tel: (0384) 78293

The Vine is the brewery tap of Bathams brewery which stands immediately next door. It is a handsome looking pub which is as characterful inside as its exterior suggests. There's a small bar to the right, and a quieter room to the left as well as other rooms to the rear which are suitable for families. The inscription at the front of the pub is from Shakespeare:

> "Blessing of your heart: You brew good ale"

Who would disagree with the statement?

The pub is also known as The Bull and Bladder on account of there being a butchers right next door (which is where the wines and spirits section is). The butcher evidently used to hang up the bladders to dry outside indicating that the meat sold was fresh! The butcher shop has long since gone but the nick-name remains to this day.

The Vine serves Batham's mild and bitter as fresh as can be, for it does not have to travel far. It is open from noon all day in the week and usual hours on Sunday. Food is available at lunchtimes on Monday to Fridays but not at weekends. The Vine is an absolute must for it is one of the very best of Black Country pubs and unspoilt, despite its popularity.

The Vine ("Bull & Bladder") – Batham's Tap

Delph Locks

Often referred to as the Nine Locks, this impressive flight is a landmark on the Black Country Canals. There is an uncertainty as to why the label "nine locks" has held for there are only eight! One other peculiarity is that they look at first glance as if there are a parallel set. These are the old locks standing alongside the new flight constructed in the 1850s. Half way up the bank you will find old stables for the canal horses standing almost as they would have been in the last century.

Buckpool and Fens Pool

The walk also leads into a nature reserve known as Buckspool and Fens Pool where reeds and marshland attract a variety of bird and plant life, so much so that the area has been designated a Site of Special Scientific Interest by the Nature Conservancy Council. These large pools are a real contrast to the truncated section of the Pensnett Canal.

The walk follows the Fens Branch to the Stourbridge Canal, built in the late 1770s to transport mainly limestone, coal and ironstone but also glassware and bricks.

The Walk

1. From the Vine descend Delph Road and go right to join the canal towpath at the Delph Bottom Lock. Climb up the locks to go under an ugly concrete bridge to the top lock. You can see a church on the hillside and also glimpses of the massive Merry Hill shopping centre.

2. Continue along the towpath of the Dudley Canal to enter a completely different world, an inland waterfront, known as The Waterfront, surrounded by offices, a hotel and all manner of eateries (in some instances American style). It seems that as

soon as you step into this unreal setting you step back out of it for around the corner the towpath reverts to a rutted path surrounded by decaying works.

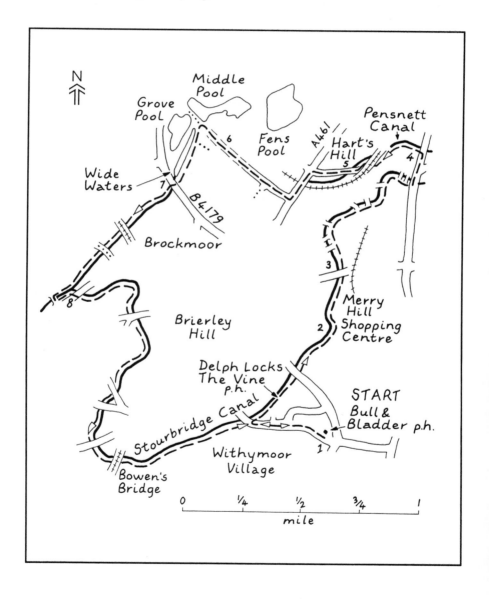

3. Follow the towpath as it winds its way to Woodside Bridge which carries the Pedmore Road. Go under the bridge then exit right and right again on the road to cross Peartree Lane. Then cross the main road wherever you can.

4. You approach the Woodside pub on the left, but beforehand turn left towards a works. Go right to join a little path along the remains of the Pensnett canal, a long lost link in the extensive canal network, which has seen better days. This is an attractor of wildlife despite its pollution and litter.

5. Follow this up to Canal Street which lives up to its name, being surrounded by engineering works no doubt some of which date from the canal era. Go right and walk to the main Dudley Road. Turn left and cross over. Before the Tap House go right along Wallows Road. As the road bends left cross over and keep ahead along a track into Buckpool and Fens pool Nature Reserve.

6. This leads to a series of pools. Fens Pool is the largest on the right, with Middle and Grove Pools ahead. They form the core of the nature reserve. The track gives out into a path which continues ahead. This reaches the pools and you turn left along a path which descends and bears right to run parallel with an old water course known as Wide Waters.

7. Cross the Pensnett Road and then regain the towpath along the canal which is now in water. Keep ahead along this section until you reach the major junction by the works. At first it looks as if there is no way to turn left but the way is by crossing at the next lock ahead and then cutting back left.

8. The Stourbridge Canal meanders considerably through Brierley Hill, a mile back to Delph Locks. Leave it here and walk back up Delph Road to the Vine along a stretch of road known as The Delph Crawl as there are so many tempting hostelries to pass by. Unless you have considerable stamina save yourself for The Vine.

21. OLD HILL

Route: Old Hill Railway Station – Station Road – Gorsty Hill Road – Coombeswood – Mucklow Hill – Leasowes Park – Dudley Canal – Old Hill Railway Station

Distance: 4 miles

Map: O.S Pathfinder Sheet 933 Stourbridge

Start: Old Hill Railway Station

Access: A half-hourly railway service to Old Hill station

Station Road is signposted off the main A459 road. There is limited parking near to the station.

The Waterfall. Tel: 021 561 3499

While there are at least six good hostelries around Old Hill railway station it is worth the ten minute walk up Waterfall Lane (left out of the station and right at the junction) to call into the Waterfall pub where there is a little waterfall in the garden. The pub has two rooms, a large lounge to the front and a cosy bar to the rear and both are friendly. One of the rooms in the pub is said to be haunted but there have been no sightings recently.

There is a good selection of real ales at any given time including Everards, Hook Norton, Marstons, and numerous guest brews. Food is served at lunch until 2.30pm and in the evening between 6pm and 9.30pm. Families are welcome and the garden is extremely popular on warm weekends. Opening times are noon until 3pm and from 5.30pm on Mondays to Fridays, all day Saturdays and usual Sunday hours. Take a walk up from the station, left down Station Road, then right into Waterfall Lane towards Blackheath and you will not be disappointed.

Leasowes Park

Bell and Bear. Tel: 021 561 2196

On the ramble you pass near to the Bell and Bear on Gorsty Hill Road, which sells Holt, Plant and Deakin ales as well as other brews. This ancient hostelry is much given over to food but nevertheless offers a fine pint of ale too. It is open all day on Monday to Fridays and from 11am – 3pm and from 6pm on Saturdays. Usual Sunday hours prevail.

If you decide to travel into Halesowen try the Waggon and Horses as it sells the excellent Mundane ales from Burton including the interestingly-named brew Opening Medicine.

Leasowes Park

The wooded parkland which features pools and trickles of streams was originally designed by William Shenstone who is said to have been one of the founding fathers of landscape gardening in England.

This type of landscaping must have been fascinating (or abhorrent) to the squatter who had settled in the area at the turn of the century. As the names of nearby settlements Blackheath and Cradley Heath suggest, this would have been open rough grassland between belts of scrub woodland. To landscape it into contrived and orderly parkland must have seemed strange at the time.

The Walk

1. Leave Oldhill Railway Station and turn right along Station Road. As it begins to climb more steeply go left up Coombes Hill. This reaches a junction where there are steps opposite which lead up to Gorsty Hill Road. Stop for a breather. You can even stop for refreshment if you wish as the Bell and Bear is only a few paces down the hill on your right.

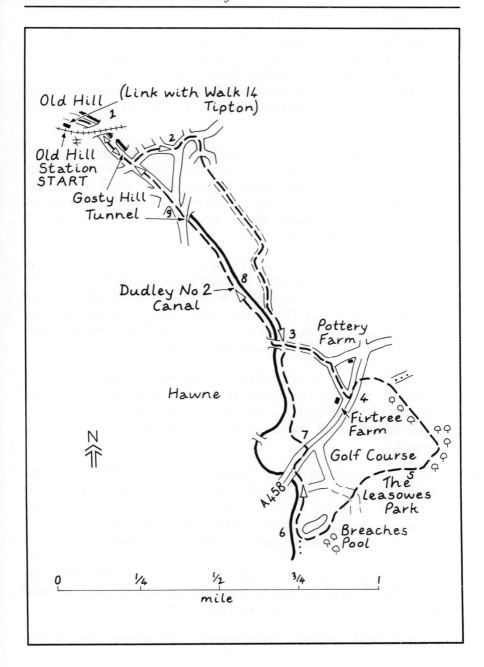

Old Hill

(Link with Walk 14 Tipton)

1

2

Old Hill Station START

Gosty Hill Tunnel

9

Dudley No 2 Canal

8

3

Pottery Farm

Hawne

4

Firtree Farm

7

Golf Course

The leasowes Park

5

A458

6

Breaches Pool

N

0   ¼   ½   ¾   1
mile

2. Cross Gorsty Hill Road and turn left to climb again but just around the corner go right down a one time access road to Coombeswood Tube works. Before the gates go left on a footpath signposted to Mucklow Hill. The way follows a fence into the valley and eventually drops down to the Dudley Canal No 2.

3. You arrive at an ornate iron bridge and at this point turn left for Mucklow Hill. Cross a stile and the path dips a little and then climbs to a stile and track. Cross another stile here and go right along the track. Before the barred gate and Firtree Farm, go left over a stile and walk on a little path to Mucklow Hill Road, a busy dual carriageway.

4. Cross with care and turn left for several metres, but go over a stile on the right signposted to Kent Road. Cross the course to a gap stile, and once through bear right following the fence as it dips down to parkland. Go right before the stream and follow it until you reach a seat and large slab of slate which reads rather poetically in the Shenstone fashion:

   "Here the path begins gradually to ascend beneath a depth of shade by the side of which is a small bubbling rill, either forming little peninsulas, rolling over pebbles, or falling down small cascades, all under cover and taught to murmur very agreeably."

5. The text reflects the very loveliness of this spot. Cross the stream here, and make a left and right. You should now be following a wide path downstream with a golf course to the left and right. This path eventually comes to a road by a pool. Cross it and descend again to come to the water's edge of Breach Pool, aptly named given the problems of breaching from the canal on more than one occasion. Follow the path around the left-hand side of the pool along a board-walk and then up steps to climb the steep embankment.

6. Turn right along the towpath along a dry section. This section

of the Dudley No 2 canal, designed by William Shenstone, is the subject of conservation. It originally extended to Selly Oak via the infamous Lapal Tunnel but the partial collapse of this structure in the 1910s brought about the canal's premature closure. On meeting the road at the car park there is no option but to rise up to Mucklow Hill Road again. Cross over and turn right to walk up to the first left turn into the industrial estate.

7. Follow the road down to what seems like a dead-end, but there between the metal fences is a path which runs through the works to eventually give out above the canal at Hawne End basin. Go left, as signposted to Quarry Hill and follow the towpath to the first footbridge which you cross. Bear left to continue walking on the towpath towards the old tube works at Coombeswood.

8. This must have been a hive of activity in earlier decades. There is a still a considerable amount of gantries and the like spanning the canal. You reach Gorsty Hill Tunnel (509 metres) but as you can see, it is a tunnel for legging only. You have to make your way quietly up the embankment. Cross a small access road and up steps to Coombes Road.

9. Cross over by the Lighthouse public house and walk down Station Road, passing two other canalside pubs, the Boat and the Wharf, on the way to the station.

22. AMBLECOTE

Route: The Moorings Tavern – Wollaston Road – Stourbridge Canal – Stourton (or return along canal)

Distance: 4 miles

Map: O.S. Pathfinder sheet 933 Stourbridge

Start: The Moorings Tavern, High Street, Amblecote

Access: Amblecote is served by regular buses from Dudley, Stourbridge and Wolverhampton.

The Moorings Tavern. Tel: (80384) 374124

The pub comprises a large room with different nooks and crannies, substantial fireplaces, and a long bar offering several real ales to choose from. As the name suggests the general theme of the pub is one of navigation. It serves beers from Bass, Tetley Bitter and Boddingtons. Fortunately, it also has a policy of stocking guest ales which change regularly.

Food is available at The Moorings from noon until 2pm and 6pm until 9pm in the evening on weekdays. A roast is available on Sunday lunch until 2.30pm. Opening times are from noon until 2.30 on weekdays (3pm on Fridays and Saturdays) and from 5pm in the evening. Usual Sunday hours prevail. There's a garden to the rear by the canalside and families are welcome.

The Bonded Warehouse

This is an interesting 18th century Grade II listed warehouse and canal basin where the Stourbridge canal now terminates. There are canal trips (mainly on Sunday afternoons) from the wharf during summer. Nearby the canal is where the *Stourbridge Lion* was manufactured in 1829, a steam locomotive which was exported for use in the USA and became known throughout the world. A trail guide, *The Lion Trail*, is available locally.

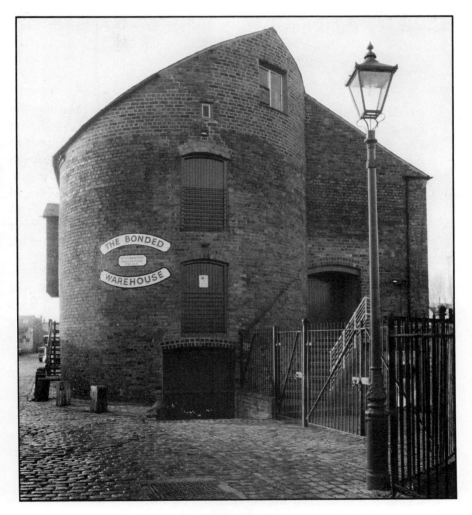

The Bonded Warehouse

Stewponey

The walk terminates at Stewponey, which is dominated by the large Stewponey Inn at a busy road junction. Across the River Stour is Stourton Castle, dating from the 14th century but mainly restored in the 19th century, hence the mock castellations. It is the birthplace of Cardinal Pole.

The Walk

1. Access to the canal is not always available by way of the Bonded warehouse so some road walking is unavoidable. From The Moorings Tavern turn left to walk along the High Street to the junction with Collis Street and Wollaston Road (also known as High Street). On your way you will notice, on the right, Holy Trinity Church where many of the great glassmakers of earlier times are buried. Turn left into Wollaston Road with Royal Doulton Crystal on the left and walk to the bridge over the canal. Turn right to join the towpath of the Stourbridge Arm or Branch canal and continue ahead.

2. The canal towpath offers an interesting insight to local works backing onto it, fittings which still exist from days when goods would have been transhipped from factory to boat. You come to Wordsley junction with the Stourbridge Canal. There's a good view up to Wordsley church from here. Cross the bridge and turn left to wander along the towpath of the Stourbridge Canal as it begins to leave the town behind.

3. At the next bridge go left over the canal and then bear right across a pasture towards Stapenhill Farm. Cross a stile into the next field and keep ahead to pass by the farm and onto a clear track. This curves around to the canal at Newton Bridge.

4. Cross the bridge to the towpath. You have a choice here. You can either go right and walk back along the canal to Stour-

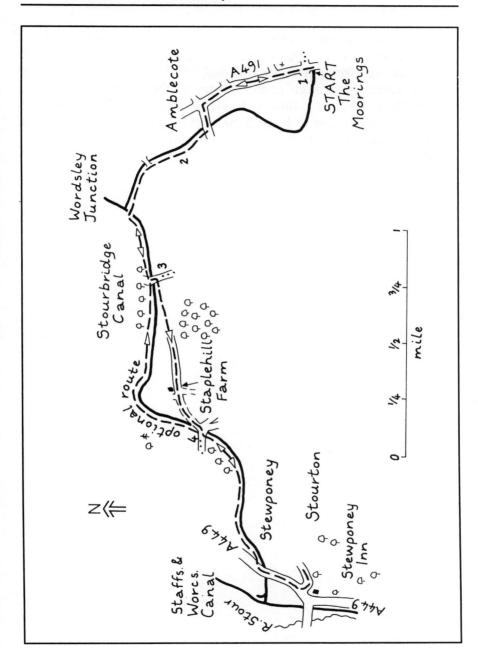

bridge or you can continue to Stourton (also known as Stewponey) and catch a bus back. My choice is for the latter given that the next section of canal is delightful, flanking a wood and then running through open country to the outskirts of Stourton. On reaching the four locks at Kidderminster Road turn left for The Stewponey, a large Banks's public house. The bus stop is 5 minutes walk on the left up the Bridgnorth Road.

23. *OLD SWINSFORD*

Route: Stourbridge Junction Railway Station — Pedmore Golf Course — Ounty John Lane — Hagley Road — Wychbury Ring — Stevens Park — Stourbridge Junction

Distance: 6 miles

Map: O.S. Sheet 933 Stourbridge

Start: Stourbridge Junction Railway Station

Access: There are regular trains to the Junction. Car travellers will find limited car parking in the area. which is on the B4186, off the A4036 Hagley Road.

The Seven Stars, Brook Road. Tel: (0384) 794483

This splendid old pub was once a Mitchells and Butler House and the brewery retained much of the tile work and woodwork for us to admire several decades later. The carved wooden back of the bar fitting is a piece de resistance. It is of impressive dimensions. There's another room and restaurant here too.

The Seven Stars serves Theakston's beers in good condition, including the unusual Theakston's Mild and for lovers of Black Country brews, Bathams bitter. It is well known in these parts for its extensive bar menu and when hot food is not available there are usually tasty rolls on the bar. Usual hours for meals are from noon until 3pm and from 5.30pm until 10pm. Families are welcome and there is a garden to the rear. In summary a first class pub which offers good hospitality to its customers.

The monument on Wychbury Hill

Wychbury

Wychbury Hill is a magical setting, the wooded slopes hiding an ancient earthwork – for early dwellers would have much preferred the high ground to their pastoral ancestors. The crumbling obelisk was built as a marker on the landscape for Hagley Hall. From here you can see across to the Clent Hills and Hagley Hall, an exceedingly good example of a Palladian Mansion dating from the 18th century. This is surrounded by landscaped parkland a project undertaken by landscape designer, Sanderson Miller.

The Walk

1. Come out of Stourbridge Junction railway station and turn left along a path until you reach a junction. Go right to climb to the left of the graveyard. The path curves right to exit onto a road. This sweeps around right by a hospice and down to the Crown public house on the Hagley Road.

2. Cross the road and turn right but then go first left into Worcester Lane. Cross to the other side and as the road curves left go over a stile on the right, the path being signposted to West Hagley. Your way is slightly left across the golf course and fortunately there are intermittent waymarker posts to guide through the flying balls. The path begins to dip down a bank. You come to a junction where you turn left to walk between trees. Exit by gardens onto Racecourse Lane.

3. Cross over to walk ahead along Ounty John Lane. This soon becomes a country lane. Continue ahead with good views across to the monument on Wychbury Hill and over to the Clent Hills with the church of Hagley in the foreground. Ounty John Lane bears right but you keep ahead through fields until you reach another junction.

4. Go left here and head towards the railway but well before the

bridge turn left (as indicated by the yellow signpost). Cross a stile by a gate and head slightly right across the field. The path now runs through rough ground to a footbridge over the railway cutting. Proceed in a similar direction to a road.

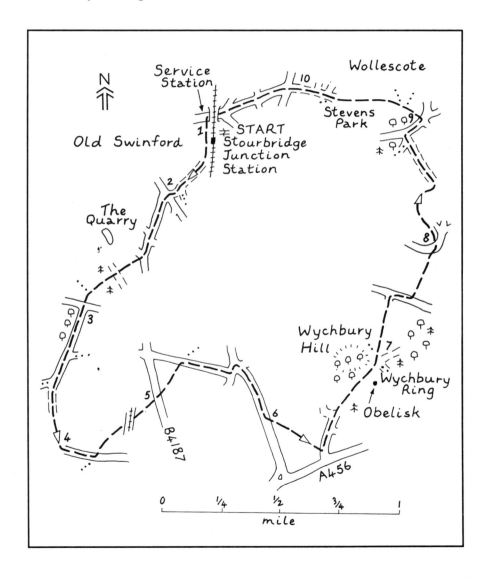

5. Cross here and walk ahead along a path to join another road. Go right and at the next main junction go left along a narrow road to join the main Hagley Road, something of a disappointment after the quietness of the preceding miles. Go right and follow the main road up to the rise of the bank and by the Prince of Wales cross the road and look for a stile on the left leading into a large field. Head slightly right, aiming for the far right corner, near a large house.

6. Go through the gateway and turn left up the narrow lane. At the top cross a stile and keep ahead to climb up the valley. The path begins to curve right to cross another stile beneath a holly bush. You can see the obelisk clearly now. The path steers its way up the bank to the left of the monument to a summit where you will find a stile leading into a tract of wood. Go through to the next stile.

7. Once over, follow the main path as it descends but take the first right along a fenced section again. This gives out onto Pedmore Lane. Go right and watch for traffic at the bend. You will see a house on the right and at this point you go through the gap on the left into a field. Follow the remnants of an old track down the field boundary (on your left) which drops down to a wood.

8. The path emerges onto Queensway Road at the edge of a housing estate. Cross the road and walk down Chalfont Place. It winds left and right then leads into Alperton Drive. Go right on Hob Green Road, turning left after the estate office into Hilltop Road where a small track on the left leads off to the rear of gardens and down the edge of a pretty little valley which has resisted the intrusion of surrounding dwellings. Go down the steps and, once across the stream, bear right to Wollescote Road.

9. Turn right and walk down to the corner. Cross the road and enter Stevens Park named after a local notable family. Do not

follow Ladybridge Brook but instead go left to rise up to the summit and then ahead towards a school. As you approach houses again, the path cuts right into a residential cul-de-sac known as The Summit. Follow this down to a junction, go left into Brackendale Way and at the bottom go left and right to skirt the school.

10.You arrive at the busy Grange Lane. Cross over to enter Grange Road and descend the hill to the Seven Stars before turning left to Stourbridge Junction.

24. NORTON (STOURBRIDGE)

Route: Norton (Broadway) – Sugar Loaf Lane – Whittington Hall Lane – Iverley Heath – Norton (Broadway)

Distance: 4 miles

Map: O.S. Pathfinder Sheet 933 Stourbridge

Start: The Broadway (Junction with Shenstone Avenue). This is where the local circular bus from Stourbridge to Norton stops.

Access: As mentioned above there is a frequent bus from Stourbridge to Norton. Those travelling by car should travel on the A451 Norton Road out of Stourbridge turning right into Greyhound Lane up to the Broadway. There is limited parking.

The Royal Exchange, Enville Street. Tel: (0384) 396726

The pub is a mile away but is near the bus route from the Broadway to Stourbridge. It is very much a locals pub but surprisingly popular with those who enjoy the outdoors. The front entrance leads to a bar on the left, with tiled floors, benches and seats around the fire. In this respect it is totally unspoilt. Food is served from noon until 2.30pm and families are welcome at this time only.

This is a Bathams house selling the elusive Bathams Mild as well as the ever popular Bitter. There's a small courtyard to the rear. The Royal Exchange is open from noon until 11pm on weekdays and usual hours on Sundays. Call in for a taste of Black Country tradition.

Stourbridge

Stourbridge is the market town for this part of the Black Country, and the central core, around High and Market Streets make for a pleasant break, although the inner ring road is a nightmare for drivers and a major barrier for pedestrians. There is a Stourbridge Architectural Heritage leaflet which highlights some of the town's finer buildings.

Glass Industry

While Stourbridge grew up as a centre for the local iron industry it also established an international reputation for first class crystal glassware. Several glassworks can be found within a couple of miles of town including the Stuart Crystal and Red House Cone Museum in High Street at Wordsley. The distinctive looking glass cone which is 100 feet high, and was built in 1790. The Cone and Victorian workshops are open to the public. Royal Doulton is passed on the Amblecote walk (in High Street) and Thomas Webb is to be found in King William Street.

The tradition of glassmaking in the area is unfolded at these factories and museums, a story which begins with the arrival of French craftsmen from Lorraine through to the rapid growth of cut glass manufacture in the 19th century. While many of the traditional glass manufacturers have now gone Stourbridge is a key centre for glass making and the "Crystal Mile" between Amblecote and Kingswinford is the core of the crystal glass business. Even the Stourbridge football club is known as the "Glassboys"!

Opposite: Stuart Crystal

The Walk

1. Walk up The Broadway and cross Sugar Loaf Lane to go left along the old Roman Road, now a track. Look for a gate on the right and Iverley Park Farm ahead. Go through the gate and the track leads directly through the farm. Keep ahead in the next field and go through a gap. The handsome farmhouse of Sugarloaf Farm stands to your right. Turn right and then at the corner left. The path rises to a junction at the top of the field. Go right to walk to Sugar Loaf Lane.

2. Turn left and walk through houses where you will see a bridleway signposted right, part of the North Worcestershire Way and a beautiful old lane to ramble. Opposite Iverley House Farm (which stands across a field on your left) go right through a gate.

3. The path keeps company with a hedge to your right. Go through a small gate and then drop left and then right along the field's edge to Turbine Cottage. Follow the drive onward to exit onto Whittington Hall Lane.

4. Go right and begin the return leg of the ramble. The road runs straight then as it bends left you go right over a stile with an appallingly defaced signpost. Head slightly right across the field, keeping to the left of old brick structures. Cross a stile and go ahead in a similar direction to a stile. Cross it and proceed along a fenced section in Iverley Heath. The path is well-worn and runs slightly right up the hillside to Sugar Loaf Lane. Turn left to return to the Broadway.

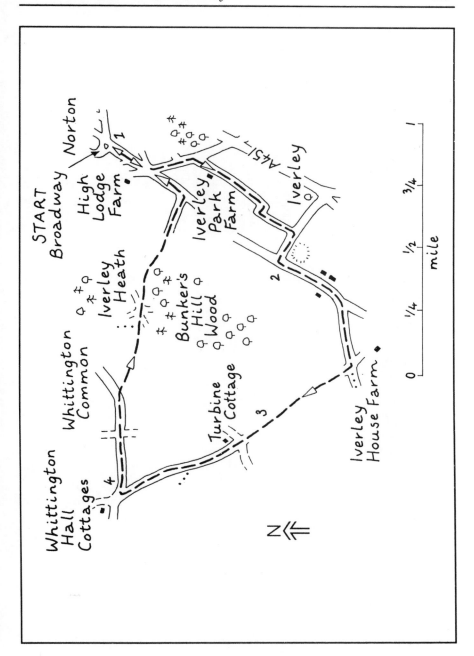

Country Walking . . .

RAMBLES IN NORTH WALES - Roger Redfern

EAST CHESHIRE WALKS - Graham Beech

WEST CHESHIRE WALKS - Jen Darling

WEST PENNINE WALKS - Mike Cresswell

STAFFORDSHIRE WALKS - Les Lumsdon

NEWARK AND SHERWOOD RAMBLES - Malcolm McKenzie

NORTH NOTTINGHAMSHIRE RAMBLES - Malcolm McKenzie

RAMBLES AROUND NOTTINGHAM & DERBY - Keith Taylor

RAMBLES AROUND MANCHESTER - Mike Cresswell

WESTERN LAKELAND RAMBLES - Gordon Brown *(£5.95)*

WELSH WALKS: Dolgellau and the Cambrian Coast
- Laurence Main and Morag Perrott *(£5.95)*

WELSH WALKS: Aberystwyth and District
- Laurence Main and Morag Perrott*(£5.95)*

WEST PENNINE WALKS - Mike Cresswell

TEASHOP WALKS IN THE CHILTERNS — Jean Patefield

WATERWAY WALKS AROUND BIRMINGHAM — David Perrott

- all of the above books are currently £6.95 each, except where indicated

Long-distance walks:

THE GREATER MANCHESTER BOUNDARY WALK - Graham Phythian

THE THIRLMERE WAY - Tim Cappelli

THE FURNESS TRAIL - Tim Cappelli

THE MARCHES WAY - Les Lumsdon

THE TWO ROSES WAY - Peter Billington, Eric Slater, Bill Greenwood and Clive Edwards

THE RED ROSE WALK - Tom Schofield

FROM WHARFEDALE TO WESTMORLAND:
historical walks through the Yorkshire Dales - Aline Watson

THE WEST YORKSHIRE WAY - Nicholas Parrott

- all £6.95 each

The Best Pub Walks!

Sigma publish the widest range of "Pub Walks" guides, covering just about every popular walking destination in England and Wales. Each book includes 25 - 30 interesting walks and varied suitable for individuals or family groups. *The walks are based on "Real Ale" inns of character and are all accessible by public transport.*

Areas covered include

Cheshire • Dartmoor • Exmoor • Isle of Wight • Yorkshire Dales • Peak District • Pennines • Lake District • Cotswolds • Mendips • Cornwall • Lancashire • Oxfordshire • Snowdonia • Devon • Northumbria • Snowdonia • Manchester

… and dozens more - all £6.95 each!

General interest:

THE INCREDIBLY BIASED BEER GUIDE - Ruth Herman
This is the most comprehensive guide to Britain's smaller breweries and the pubs where you can sample their products. Produced with the collaboration of the Small Independent Brewers' Association and including a half-price subscription to The Beer Lovers' Club. *£6.95*

DIAL 999 - EMERGENCY SERVICES IN ACTION - John Creighton
Re-live the excitement as fire engines rush to disasters. See dramatic rescues on land and sea. Read how the professionals keep a clear head and swing into action. **£6.95**

THE ALABAMA AFFAIR - David Hollett
This is an account of Britain's rôle in the American Civil War. Read how Merseyside dockyards supplied ships for the Confederate navy, thereby supporting the slave trade. The *Alabama* was the most famous of the 'Laird Rams', and was chased half way across the world before being sunk ignominiously. *£6.95*

PEAK DISTRICT DIARY - Roger Redfern
An evocative book, celebrating the glorious countryside of the Peak District. The book is based on Roger's popular column in *The Guardian* newspaper and is profusely illustrated with stunning photographs. *£6.95*

I REMAIN, YOUR SON JACK - J. C. Morten (edited by Sheila Morten)
A collection of almost 200 letters, as featured on BBC TV, telling the moving story of a young soldier in the First World War. Profusely illustrated with contemporary photographs. *£8.95*

FORGOTTEN DIVISIONS - John Fox
A unique account of the 1914 - 18 War, drawing on the experience of soldiers and civilians, from a Lancashire town and a Rhineland village. The book is well illustrated and contains many unique photographs. *£7.95*

ROAD SENSE - Doug Holland

A book for drivers with some experience, preparing them for an advanced driving test. The book introduces a recommended system of car control, based on that developed by the Police Driving School. Doug Holland is a highly qualified driving instructor, working with RoSPA. *£5.95*

TRAINING THE LEARNER DRIVER - Don Gates

The essential guide for all those intending to teach a friend or relation to drive. Written by a drivng professional so that you'll know that you are teaching just the same way as a driving instructor. *£6.95*

WE ALSO PUBLISH:

A new series of investigations into the Supernatural, Myth and Magic:

GHOSTS, TRADITIONS AND LEGENDS OF OLD LANCASHIRE
- Ken Howarth *(£7.95)*

SHADOWS: A northern investigation of the unknown
- Steve Cliffe *(£7.95)*

MYSTERIES OF THE MERSEY VALLEY
- Jenny Randles and Peter Hough *(£7.95)*

Plus, superb illustrated books on Manchester's football teams:

RED FEVER! From Rochdale to Rio as United Supporters *(£7.95)*

MANCHESTER UNITED - Moments to Remember *(£6.95)*

MANCHESTER CITY - Moments to Remember *(£9.95)*

Many more entertaining and educational books are being regularly added to our list. All of our books are available from your local bookshop. In case of difficulty, or to obtain our complete catalogue, please contact:

Sigma Leisure,
1 South Oak Lane, Wilmslow, Cheshire SK9 6AR

Phone: 0625 - 531035 Fax: 0625 - 536800

ACCESS and VISA orders welcome - call our friendly sales staff or use our 24 hour Answerphone service! Most orders are despatched on the day we receive your order - you could be enjoying our books in just a couple of days.